# St. Andrews Rock

# ST. ANDREWS ROCK

*The State of the Church
in Scotland*

*Edited by Stewart Lamont*

**Bellew Publishing**
London
1992

First published in Great Britain in 1992 by
Bellew Publishing Company Limited
8 Balham Hill, London SW12 9EA

ISBN 1 85725 046 X

Phototypeset by Intype, London
Printed and Bound in Great Britain by
Hartnolls Limited, Bodmin, Cornwall.

# Contents

# Introduction

In 1300, the country which today is called Scotland was still struggling to assert a national identity. Out of a melting pot of Gaels, Picts, Scots and Northumbrians had emerged a nation of half a million people which had soon found itself in conflict with its larger neighbour to the south. Leaderless after the execution of Wallace, the Scots found a champion in King Robert Bruce whose victory in 1314 at the battle of Bannockburn consolidated his kingdom. At the same time as this new nation emerged on the European scene, the vast cathedral on the east coast at St. Andrews was nearing completion, a monument to the pretensions of this small medieval town which soon became the ecclesiastical capital of Scotland. The tiny horse-shoe harbour bustled with traffic from Europe, while above it, on the cliffs overlooking the North Sea, the cathedral dominated the town. Despite its ruined state, it still dominates, but the cliffs have been eroded by the tides and skeletal fingers of land extend into the North Sea. It has become a paradigm of Scots religion – evoking past glories rather than things to come. Its grey stones once looked down on princes of the Church and the Protestants who supplanted them, but, despite the strong foundations that both had built within the Scottish nation, the tide has been irresistible. For seven hundred years, Christianity – in Catholic and Protestant varieties – sustained the State of Scotland. It no longer does so. That is the bleak reality as the churches of Scotland approach the millennium. The reasons for this can be debated, the suggested remedies are various, but the sad reality is that the territory which the tide of secularism has eroded is unlikely to be reclaimed.

This is far from saying that Scottish Christianity is dead, or that the religious faith which sustained it has been extinguished. However, the form which that faith takes in the twenty-first century will surely be radically different. State enforcement of multi-culturalism in schools has dealt a death-blow to the notion that Scotland is a Christian country. Already there are head teachers who will not celebrate the festivals of the Christian year in case they offend ethnic minorities. Roman Catholic state schools have stood outside this process, but I suspect that they will not survive into the next century and the Catholic Church will feel the choking effects of having a ready supply of young communicants denied to them. They are already experiencing the same sharp decline which has affected the Established Church which has gone from 1.3 million adult members in 1961 to three-quarters of a million in 1991, while the Scottish population has remained at around 5 million. To have lost between a third and a half of your membership in one generation is bad enough, but when you examine future trends (young communicants and infant baptisms), they suggest that when the present generation of church-going senior citizens has passed on, there will be precious few to replace them.

The purpose of this book is not to bemoan this decline or wallow in despair. Time will decide the form in which Christianity survives in Scotland, as undoubtedly it will. Those who read this book will, I suspect, be among those who wish it to survive. Perhaps they will feel that my analysis so far has been over-pessimistic, another prophecy of doom. My answer would be that, as a journalist, I learned that duty to truth means telling things as they are, rather than as we might wish them to be. However, I hope that after reading the contributions to this book the conclusion of the reader will be that Scots Christianity is evolving rather than becoming extinct.

Of course, there are many congregations which seem to be immune from the decline affecting most of the mainstream churches. They do so by offering charismatic worship or doctrinal certainties. While it may satisfy those who embrace it, and be successful in attracting converts, especially as the feeling grows that we are nearing a turning-point in human history in the year 2000, this type of religion is unlikely to capture the minds of the majority of the Scottish people and will remain on the fringe of social developments. Its counterpart – the liberal/moderate mind-set – has demonstrably failed to deliver the goods and it is easy to sympathize with the conservative evangelical who looks at his full pews and asks why the church up the road is not following his example. The answer to that is not simply that the declining church is being perverse or weak in faith; granting intellectual integrity to both of them, we must simply conclude that they represent different types of faith which are able to be reconciled only behind paradox or a very generous definition of Christian unity.

When the ecumenical movement began, it seemed to imply that behind the diverse dogmas there was a holy compromise or the revelation of some absolute truth which could put an end to the proud assertions of some denominations that they alone had been granted the divine version of the faith. A generation on, that hope seems just as far off, and perhaps in retrospect a little naive. On the positive side there is now a great deal more respect for other traditions, some understanding of why they believe as they do, and not a little good-will. These are gains. But along with them comes the realization that AD 2000 will pass without Christian unity assuming organic form. The talk has now switched to 'unity amid diversity' and it has not stopped at Christianity. Pluralism or multi-faith diversity has enlarged the melting pot.

That is where this book comes in. It does not attempt to balance Christianity and other religions in Scotland. It looks predominantly at the Protestant picture and the self-critical debate which is going on as the Kirk contemplates the twenty-first century. But the diversity of the contributors' thinking is sufficient to rank as a kind of pluralism in itself. Johnston R. Mckay's pessimism about the future of Presbyterianism is balanced by R. D. Kernohan's attempt to argue that the Kirk need not die. Andrew Herron traces the way the Kirk was financed in the past and wistfully admits that things can never be the same again. Ian Mackenzie's oblique look at the poverty of intellect in the modern Kirk is perhaps reinforced by the essay by one of the Kirk's great intellects Thomas F. Torrance, who looks back with not a little anger at what the present generation has done with the legacy of the Victorians. Yet Elizabeth Templeton is content to live with the frustrating conflict of loyalties in her love/hate relationship with the institutional Church. William Still remains convinced that the Kirk's salvation lies in biblical expository preaching; yet one of the pulpit giants, Murdo Ewen Macdonald seems to seek a more social gospel. The two bishops of the Episcopal Church (Richard Holloway and Michael Hare Duke) offer complementary essays reflecting both the caring and authority roles of the Church which belie the bogeyman reputation that bishops have had from within the Kirk.

Bill Shaw's sermon has much to say about the religious temperament of Scotland when it deals with our failure to take risks. Principal Shaw was a lawyer who became a theologian, but the conclusion of the book is left to a lawyer whose grasp of theology betrays his devout upbringing. Lord Mackay of Clashfern was a unique choice for the office of Lord Chancellor, the first Free Presbyterian to have held it. His reflections on the mutual responsibilities of church and state are not only highly relevant but rooted in the scriptures.

Theology is very cliquey. Collections of theological essays usually reflect a consensus or the bias of the editor. I hope this book will be considered an exception in the breadth of its contributions. But don't expect everything. I am well aware that many strands of Christianity are missing. Feminist theology; radical movements which support stronger political involvement by Christians; charismatics who practise 'power evangelism' or 'spirit led' worship – all these have gained in support in recent years and yet do not feature in this book. It is not simply lack of sympathy for their beliefs which has caused their omission. They represent a recurrent trend in Scots Protestantism of revivals or secessions from the main body which thrive on the fringe of the national church. Their appeal is limited to a minority and will, in my opinion, remain so. The question is not whether one of these 'ginger' groups will take over and dominate the national church, but whether it can survive at all in the role of a body which represents a broad spectrum of theologies and forms of worship without acute tensions developing.

Put another way, the question is whether the centre can hold when pulled in divergent ways by groups who claim to have the answer to the Kirk's sagging membership roll and general indifference towards organized religion in a secular society. The Kirk could end up as a coalition of minorities, most of which have little in common. Those who want an evangelical revival are irrevocably opposed to New Age movements. Those who refuse to wear robes and have parishes in peripheral housing estates are deeply suspicious of the values of the more comfortable suburbs. There were always conflicting views within the national Kirk, but there was cohesion because of the force of authority which the Kirk claimed for itself through its courts. Now everything is up for grabs. Doctrine, practice and procedure are all in flux. It is difficult to predict what kind of church will emerge in Scotland next century, but in my view it will either be a shrunken Kirk with a more conservative evangelical stance, or else a loose association of worshipping groups which are influenced by the community in which they are set.

The 'super-church' which ecumenical enthusiasts of a generation ago had envisaged is unlikely to come about. The stance (and legacy through the bishops he has appointed) of Pope John Paul II has ensured that there are unlikely to be any moves for church unity of an organizational nature. There is plenty of goodwill between the Kirk and the Roman Catholic Church especially at local level, but despite the latter joining the new national ecumenical body ACTS, there are still formidable differences on issues such as women clergy, mixed marriages and inter-communion which will ensure that changes in both churches will take place in parallel rather than jointly. That is partly the reason (and apology) that this volume is confined to the situation on the Reformed side of the fence. The Roman Catholic Church is not without its problems, but Scottish Protestants can usually find enough to argue about among themselves without re-running the battles of yesteryear. We remain (and will remain) a pluralistic religious nation who enjoy finding fault in ourselves and in our neighbour's theology.

I must say that I agree with Ron Ferguson's sentiments that we have now reached the point where it ought to be possible for Protestants and Catholics to be rude to one another about important issues without the ecumenical movement packing up its tent and going off in a huff. Alas, the reality is that many cracks have been papered over and any progress at leadership level on touchy issues such as mixed marriages and inter-communion has been very little in the twenty years during which I have been writing on religious affairs. Fortunately, many ordinary members have been more willing to take risks than their hierarchs, and thanks to them Scotland has never looked like becoming another Ulster. The cuddling up between the SNP and the Catholic church at the expense of the 'pro-abortion' Labour party in the 1992 election, illustrates the scotticising trend among west-coast Catholics which will ensure that religious differences are unlikely to become entrenched in political parties.

Andrew Herron tells a story about the shipwrecked Scotsman rescued from an uninhabited desert island who had built himself a church. As the rescue vessel pulled away, they spotted another little church across the bay. His rescuers knew that he had been alone on the island, so why the other church, they asked. 'That is the church I don't go to,' replied the pugnacious Scot, illustrating a characteristic that has been part of Scottish religious history. Do not expect to find agreement among the contributors to this book but you will find prophetic pointers to the way that Scottish Christianity will develop. Amid the glistening pebbles left behind by the sea of faith in ebb-tide, you may find the runes of a church for the twenty-first century.

STEWART LAMONT

# Chapter 1

# Why I Love and Hate the Church

Elizabeth Templeton

*Elizabeth Templeton taught theology at the University of Edinburgh but following marriage and motherhood has become a 'freelance theologian' an innovative role which won her invitations to address the 1988 Lambeth Conference and the 1990 World Council of Churches Assembly in Canberra. She has recently begun the Threshold theological resource project (a drop-in centre in Edinburgh for those who seek to explore) and become editor of Trust, SCM's newsletter for those who sit loose to orthodoxy or organized religion.*

A few weeks ago, I had occasion to be lunching with a Roman Catholic priest to arrange a meeting. He mentioned that he would be saying mass immediately beforehand, and that I was welcome to attend if I wanted.

Having learned to be twitchy about ecumenical protocol after years of negotiating the diplomacies of inter-church eucharists, I was not clear what this meant. So just before the service I asked him whether, being there, I should receive the elements or not.

His answer, though generously meant, filled me with horror: 'If you'd like to, you're welcome to receive. Nobody here knows you, so you won't be a cause of scandal.'

I hate the Church for being so bad at manifesting the generosity of God, who would, I think, have omitted the second sentence! As it happened, the priest was wrong. There *was* someone there who knew me, a woman whom I'd met in her professional context without ever having known anything about her religious background. As it happened too, she was the one who took up the offertory gifts, and I knew she must have seen me there.

I *did* receive, partly because I felt the need to offer my tangle of pity, anger and scorn at the state of the Church in the hope of its transformation into something creative. And partly I because now find the differences between the denominational forms of communion relatively superficial, and as a baptized Christian I am sure

I *belong* to this eucharistic community, despite all the dividing ink and sometimes blood that lie behind us and between us.

At the end, I wanted to say thank you to the woman who'd been, so to speak, part of the hospitality. So I followed her out and said it was nice to see her, that it had meant something to me that she'd been part of the service. To my amazement, her eyes filled with tears. It transpired that she had, for eighteen years now, been going to mass without receiving communion, because many years ago, when she married a Presbyterian, her then priest had said to her: 'You might as well have married a pagan. Don't take communion again.' She, in obedience and pain, had never challenged that ban, and had sat there unfed, while I, in my ecumenical gluttony, ate!

Such nonsenses are not the monopoly of one denomination; nor is this a piece of anti-Roman propaganda. I have encountered analogous abuses among smug Protestants discussing whether Roman Catholics count as Christians at all; and the complacencies and exclusions of our past take multi-denominational forms.

Sometimes they are not even to do with theology (or not on the surface). As a student, I attended a conference at Scottish Churches House. On the Sunday morning, Bobby, one of the American students decided to go to the cathedral. This was in the late 1960s, when ragged jeans and long hair were *de rigueur*. Again, it turned out to be communion. But as he approached the door, a frock-coated elder said to him, as his first words: 'Have you come to the right place?' Bobby, fortunately, was a robust soul. 'Is this a Christian church?' he said. And, on receiving an affirmative answer: 'Well, I've come to the right place.'

Such crass failure to enact the catholic messianic invitation to men and women and children who come from North and South, and East and West is woeful. We expect the *world* to map itself out in exclusion zones of race, wealth, class, education and so on, but for the *Church* to emulate and even pioneer such exclusions is so sad and sickening that I am often tempted to write it off as irredeemable.

That, of course, would be bad theology, and self-righteous to boot, since I reckon that the multiple failures of the Church's life are magnifications of our own capacity for what the trade calls 'sin'. But besides that, where else is there to go? There is no attraction for me in sectarian purities of doctrine or practice: it's catholicity or nothing. And the reason why I *love* the Church is that it has actually been the milieu in which my vision of the largeness of God has grown. It is where I taste desire for the transfiguration of things, and hear it affirmed and deepened. Ironically, without the Church, I couldn't hate the Church; one has to treat almost with tenderness a body which so signals its own failure by constantly reaffirming the criteria by which to judge it – love, truth, freedom, grace.

It is not the *failing* I hate. Self-forgiveness is an implicate of gospel for community as for particular persons. In a funny way, I *expect* the Church to fail, being more at home with a Lutheran sense of the Church as *'simul iustus et peccator'* than with an orthodox sense of its sinlessness. What is insufferable is that so often it seems to be precisely those things which ought to be confused which are celebrated! The near-standard dissociation from the whole realm of sexuality; the near-uniform 'niceness' of church life, beneath which animosities fester rather than being faced, and possibly transcended, with candour; the insistent pride in confessional positions which we should be offering as grubby and tattered failures to articulate the truth of God in ways which open it to others.

Archie Craig once commented on the impact of a dreary procession in Sauchiehall Street where a group of bedraggled and ill-assorted men shambled along under sandwich boards proclaiming eternal life. It is that kind of mismatch which seems so palpable when we get a momentary glimpse of our church life as it strikes the outsider: boring, predictable, self-preoccupied, moralistic, unimaginative, under sandwich boards proclaiming the Fruits of the Spirit.

And yet . . .

And yet, I have had glimpses of what it means for the Church to be an anticipation of the Kingdom of God. I have seen a friend whose living-room was bright with an Advent wreath when a Jewish acquaintance came to visit. And almost without thinking she brought out three other candles so that he could be included rather than excluded from the light. I have watched the courtesy of ecumenically mellow men and women with one another's customs, giving maximum space and attentiveness to ways not their own, and yet without servility or nervousness. I have heard a wonderful Benedictine nun speak about truthfulness in her rule, and about the potentially lethal hypocrisy of official 'religious' life. When there was a dispute in the convent, a characteristic mode of making it up would be for one sister to say to another: 'I know you didn't mean to hurt my feelings, but . . .' 'Damn it,' said this robust and tranquil woman: 'I want the credit for being nasty when I'm trying to be.'

Now it may be simply that there is, across the human race, such a distribution of temperamental grace that any community, of any faith or none, will contain a proportion of people whose wisdom, sanity, humour, steadiness and integration is conspicuous. Certainly, I can do no arithmetical sleight-of-hand which conjures statistics to suggest that Christianity produces a greater number of such people per head of its population than any other faith. Indeed, I hear with serious concern that such an analysis suggests that a disproportionate number of authoritarian personalities are attracted to the Church. Yet I must say that when I look at the galaxies of people who have interpreted to me what the gospel is, interpreted it by *being* it, most have been deeply implicated in the Church's life, to the point of inseparability. And I love the Church for their being there.

This is no argument from quantity. Indeed, it is no argument at all, for even the quality can be read as accidental or, worse, as existing and surviving in spite of the Church rather than because of it. But I am haunted by the Johannine suggestion that 'we do not know what we shall be, but we shall be like him, for we shall see him as he is'. And the congruence between the sort of open, tough, generous personhood which searches mine and the Christology they live out of is striking.

So I continue to live with this institution, loving it and hating it at the same time, and with a sense of there being nowhere else to go. At times I am so moved by the potential creativity of it all, by a sense of communion across boundaries of race, sex, culture and tradition that I could weep for the beautiful openness of it. At times I am so appalled by the triumphalism, the barbaric inattentiveness to secular culture, the parochial complacency that I can practically feel us being spat out of God's mouth!

How to live with both these responses simultaneously, with integrity, is probably my main existential question – or at least the main one for public consumption. On the one hand I have friends – wonderful, colourful, bold people full of energy and passion – who cannot understand why anyone who has not already suffered soul-death sits on church committees, deals with the institutional bureaucracy, spends time on questions of credal formulation or thinks formal ecumenical activity worth a fig. On the other hand I have friends – wonderful, faithful, full of amazing patience – who have devoted their lives to the slow conversations involved in faith and order issues between denominations, and who find the quick camaraderie of supercilious activists painful and unfinished. I marvel at them both, and am pulled by the polar attractions of both. But retaining any sense of equilibrium is, to put it mildly, like trying to live with the sun and the moon at the same time. On one level, one knows they are both really there, all the time, and vital to the earth's functioning. But in terms of how one defines days and nights, it is an either/or. Pale moons may inhabit the daytime sky, but 'day' is when the sun is dominant and night is when the sun might as well not be 'there', since it can shed neither heat nor light on the situation.

I find it hard to get perspective on this. But I am convinced that if the vast themes of reconciliation and redemption are to be earthed convincingly, neither pole can be eliminated. The primary difficulty in the Church at present – and that in almost every denomination – is the tendency to withdraw from engagement with what is most difficult, challenging, 'other', into a kind of ghetto: fundamentalism.

Nor is this the prerogative of the theologians of conservative tendency, whether Roman Catholic, Protestant or indeed of faiths other than Christian. In every faith community, liberals and radicals find it increasingly difficult to communicate with their *own* conservatives, and often find it easier to cross denominational or inter-faith boundaries with those who recognizably share the same willingness to relate, than to cope with those in their own group who oppose such contact. And it is a clear option, voiced by some at the radical pole and some at the conservative one, that life would be easier if we simply split.

For me, the lovableness of the Church is to do with that *not* happening. For such a split would signal the reduction of reconciliation to natural like-mindedness and opting out of the tough wrestling for truth which can happen only when people believe significantly different things or live in significantly different ways. It is the fidelity to a vision of communion which transcends difference, and where we learn that we cannot be ourselves without one another, which stretches me with desire and challenge. Any ecumenism which is reduced to prudence or self-preservation seems to me a trivializing and betraying of that breathtaking sense of inter-relatedness which nerves all creative love. Ever since I first came across it in Hooker's sermon 'On Pride', I have been haunted by one of his sentences: 'God hath created nothing simply for itself, but each thing in all things: and of everything each part in other have such interest, that in the whole world nothing is found whereunto any thing created can say: "I need thee not".' In a sense, it is simply Paul's body-metaphor again. But its extension to everything in creation seems to me to add to the sense of the Church as that community called to be a microcosm of the unity of all things, not just a detachable sub-section of the world's larger reality.

This is the ultimate stretching ecumenism which calls us into conversation with everyone else: people of other faiths, the secular world, the past, the future, the alien, the marginal, the voiceless. Too often the Church turns it back on this invitation, settling for a more sectarian sense of its own identity. But I love the Church which still enacts the courage and risk of such exploring openness, often crossing boundaries which scare many of those back at the ranch.

I began this essay with a vignette of the Church as I hate it, trapped in its past, untranscendent, wrestling with its own legalism. Strangely, the same church has recently given me a polar opposite image of its lovely creative imagination working at its best. I have read no comment on whether the priest involved was castigated for liturgical impropriety, but he is a true example of the Church incarnating the freeing love of God.

The story appears in *Seven for a Secret* (SPCK, 1991), where Tracy

Hensen tells of the sexual abuse she suffered as a child, the long slow process of coming to terms with it and how she learned to accept herself. It is the enacted acceptance of her reception into the Church which is the culmination of her healing. But what struck me most was that, to reach the depth of her past disassociation from herself, the priest also went through a baptismal ceremony with a doll which, since her childhood, had represented her unclean, unacceptable self. That he would risk sentimentality, ridicule, theological opprobrium (things without souls cannot be baptized), having grasped the need for a symbol which would heal the splits of the past, and that he had the courage to *play* as a mode of expressing it, seems to me wonderful.

I suppose such sorts of minor atonement happen all the time: glimpses of redeemed and generous community among so much that is crass, sluggish and lethally introverted, wounding rather than healing, reinforcing human apartheids rather than breaking them down. Whether or not they vindicate my love of the Church in the face of the bulk of awfulness it carries in its luggage depends, I suppose, on how you understand atonement. In that sense, I think, loving the Church is not a natural but a supernatural act, depending on the confidence that Christ opens for it a future which transfigures the solid and sullied past.

At any rate, I expect to have to go on living with my chaos of responses, love, hate, anger, pity, tenderness, dismay, amazement, horror, marvelling, hope, dread. The love, I hope, will have the last word, but not easily – certainly not obviously.

When I am most tempted to despair, I meditate sometimes on the deep paradox of Edwin Morgan's 'The Fifth Gospel' and take comfort:

> Listen: a sower went out to sow. And when he sowed, some seeds fell by the wayside, and they sprang up and gave good fruit. Some fell on stony places, where they had not much earth, and they too grew up and flourished well. And some fell among thistles, and they in turn sprang and gave fruit in the very heart of the thistles. But others fell into good ground, and died, and produced neither leaf nor fruit. (*From Glasgow to Saturn*, Carcanet, 1973)

Chapter 2

# Crisis in the Kirk

## Thomas F. Torrance

*Thomas F. Torrance was born in pre-revolutionary China to a missionary family which has played a significant role in shaping theological opinion in the twentieth-century Kirk. Arguably Scotland's major theologian this century, he held his first Chair in the University of Edinburgh in Ecclesiastical History before becoming Professor of Christian Dogmatics. A neo-Barthian, he won the international Templeton prize for his work relating theology and science and was Moderator of the General Assembly in 1976. Now living in retirement, he has never hesitated to speak out if he thought doctrinal orthodoxy or standards were being undermined and this contribution is an extended version of a series of articles he contributed to* Life and Work *in 1990–91.*

## The Crisis of Faith

A few years ago, in a discussion about belief with Professor J.K.S. Reid, one of our finest theologians, I asked what he thought of the Church of Scotland today. He answered at once: 'It breaks my heart.' What a change has come about since the renewal of belief in the great truths of the gospel in which he took part before and after the Second World War. We have seen a retreat from the high ground of doctrinal certainties to the low ground of socio-political utilitarianism without much evangelical substance. In preparing his economic survey of the Church of Scotland in 1977 the late Professor Nathaniel Wolfe made a point of stressing to me that the root problem in the state of the Kirk had to do with a crisis of faith. I found it startling that such a judgement should be made by a Jew who was not himself much of a believer but who was deeply saddened by what his own analysis of the Church of Scotland brought to light. Only a recovery of belief, he insisted, would reverse the steady decline in the life and membership of the Kirk.

When I read several of the reports to the General Assembly in May 1986 I wondered whether a return to central Christian beliefs was on the way. I found the biblical and theological arguments of the Board of Social Responsibility particularly heartening, while the *Statement of Christian Faith* submitted by the Panel on Doctrine, in spite of its muted terms, marked a real step forward. Even the report of the Church and Nation Committee registered a deeper concern for biblical teaching in the face of its regular tendency to slant Christian convictions towards current ideological trends.

By and large, however, little attention is given throughout the Church to the primary truths of the gospel, for a rejection of belief in the supernatural seems to have set in, together with a secular way of thinking that discounts God's direct action in revelation and history. As a result, people's confidence in the truth and authority of the Holy Scriptures is undermined, and a steady erosion of the gospel is found in the preaching and teaching the Church. Many ministers are often little more than servants of public opinion, who take their cue from the newspapers, with only incidental reference to the Bible, and offer to their congregations insipid sermons concocted from confused second-hand ideas. Obsession for relevance has led to a detachment of Christianity from Christ, and its attachment to society, so that the Christian way of life is reinterpreted to make it endorse the cheap humanistic philosophies of life placarded before our eyes by film and television. Christianity is reduced to being not much more than the sentimental religious froth of a popular socialism – the 'cheese and cookies notion of Christianity'. What Americans call 'car bumper theologies' replace the distinctive doctrines of the Christian faith, and trendy substitute-religions replace strong evangelical witness to Jesus Christ as Lord and Saviour.

What lies behind all this? Much of it has to be traced back to the corrupting effect of sociological habits of thought rooted in a split culture that have been absorbed by the Church in a desire to enhance its social image. This has been happening in the very years when current social sciences have been castigated by leading scientists like Lord Porter, the President of the Royal Society, for their pseudo-scientific methods and explanations. The tragedy is that the more churchmen and theologians climb on to the bandwagon of these backward social sciences, the more irrelevant their preaching and teaching become and the gap between the Church and spiritually hungry people continues to widen. How really relevant is the Church to the modern world? Not one of our theological faculties offers any course on the inter-relation of theology and science in the training of our ministers, with the result that pseudo-scientific ideas are rife in our theological colleges. Thus the 'historico-critical scientific method' pursued by our biblical scholars is governed by obsolete preconceptions, such as their notion of time, upon which scientists today pour scorn, but to which many scholars still cling, for they seem unwilling to face the pain of change in their sceptical and outmoded habits of thought.

An immense revolution has taken place in our science. Gone is the closed determinist conception of the universe with its mechanistic explanations that excluded any thought of God's interaction with the world, and rejected miraculous or supernatural events as a 'violation of natural law'. Is it not that obsolete conception that lies behind the sceptical attitude of people to the Virgin Birth or the bodily Resurrection of Jesus, or his miraculous acts of healing? John Polkinghorne, the Cambridge scientist, writes that he has no difficulty in believing in what the Bible tells us about the birth and resurrection of Jesus, and claims that the so-called 'nature miracles', set aside by many scholars, are precisely what he would expect of one who is the incarnate Word of God through whom all things are created and given their rational order. The basic question here is whether we really believe in the deity of Jesus Christ or not.

Several times in its history the Church has struggled for the essential truth of the gospel when the deity of Christ was at stake. The first struggle culminated in the fourth century when the Nicene Creed was formulated which states that Jesus Christ is 'of one substance with the Father'. Unless there is an unbroken relation in being between Christ and God then what he reveals of God the Father has no divine validity. Unless his saving activity is identical with God's activity, then the gospel message of reconciliation, forgiveness and eternal life is empty of divine reality. Unless Jesus Christ is the incarnate Son of God in whom we meet and know God himself, and unless he lived and died for us and our salvation, and rose again in body from the dead, all that the gospel tells us is finally only of passing symbolic significance and irrelevant to human beings in space and time. The second occasion when such a struggle took place was at the Reformation. Here too it was the absolute centrality of Jesus Christ in revelation and salvation that was at stake. Unless he is identical with the self-revelation of God, we cannot believe that God is really like Jesus, and unless Jesus Christ is God come to save us, we cannot believe that it is God himself who forgives and justifies us by his grace. Is it not the same struggle that we have today with an insidious secularism undermining saving belief in Christ as the Son of God? Do we really believe in the Incarnation or not, and believe not just in some symbolic way but in a real and honest way?

Here we put our finger on the pulse of the Church's faith. When people talk about 'incarnational Christianity', do they mean anything more than the relation of spirit and matter? When they speak about the resurrection, do they think of it only in some sort of symbolic way and not as a real act of God in space and time? These are crucial issues. When scholars think of the incarnation in a mythological way or churchmen agree with the Bishop of Durham's rejection of the physical resurrection of Jesus in favour of some sort of spiritual resurrection, it is evident that once again the very essence of the Christian gospel is at stake. How tragic it is, then, for such people to deride evangelical believers in the truth of the biblical revelation as 'fundamentalists', and to want to marginalize them in the life of the Kirk although they are the staunchest supporters of its historic Reformed Faith!

No branch of the Church has ever survived when it has retreated from the absoluteness and centrality of Christ and lapsed from the evangelical truths of the gospel. How could it when these truths belong to the very essence of Christ's Church? Without evangelical belief the heart goes out of the Church and its membership dwindles away, as is happening now so rapidly in Scotland. The more the distinctive doctrines of divine revelation are set aside in the obsession of the Church to be socially relevant, the further the Church disappears into secular society. To take seriously our Lord's assertion that he was sent to proclaim the gospel to the poor, means that we must be concerned to bring the specifically Christian gospel of salvation through Christ to bear upon all humanitarian and social need. But the downgrading of the fundamental truths of the gospel results in a rampant secularization in which the difference between the message of the Church and the message of social utilitarianism is wiped out. What we desperately need today is a biblical and Christological revolution in our theology, and that means a radical change in the minds of theologians, ministers and elders, as well as in the general membership of our congregations throughout the land. Unless we allow the incarnate and risen Lord and Saviour to be the very centre of our lives and thought, and unless we believe unreservedly in the divine efficacy of the gospel, the crisis pointed out by Nat Wolfe will inevitably lead to the decimation of the Kirk. Let us hope that the biblical and theological ingredients in the reports to the General Assembly, to which I referred at the beginning, really indicate a turning-point in the Kirk toward the renewal of biblical teaching and evangelical doctrine.

## The Crisis of Morality

In some of our older churches one can see behind the pulpit or behind the communion table two murals on which are inscribed the Ten Commandments and the Creed. That derives from an old Reformed tradition in which 'the Law' and 'the Belief' were combined with one another in the evangelical teaching and preaching of the Church. Upright behaviour and doctrinal convictions were closely linked together in the daily life of God's people through personal commitment to Jesus Christ as Lord and Saviour. By and large, today that evangelical connection has been severed, and this has given rise to an alarming collapse in private and public morality over the last twenty or thirty years.

There has been an enormous increase in crimes of violence and robbery, frequently fuelled by drugs and alcohol, and often ruthlessly organized, together with a demonic delight in cruelty to human beings and animals. What is most distressing is the growth of crimes against the person and the degradation of humanity made in the image of God. This is everywhere evident in our society in a catastrophic breakdown in family relations, domestic brutality, the corruption of parenthood, the prevalence of promiscuity, adultery and divorce, incest and child abuse, single parent families, the alienation of children from parents, the enormous increase in teenage vagrancy and prostitution and suicide, the widely accepted practice of extra-marital fornication together with abortion on demand, the horrific wickedness of pornography and the abominable exploitation by men and women of infants and children in the gratification of perverted sex, sometimes mixed with the cultivation of the black arts and even ritual human sacrifice in the worship of the devil.

All this adds up to an unprecedented crisis in morality: it is no answer to blame governments and their policies, for in daily life (and especially in education) there has been a disastrous slump in the impact of Christian teaching upon the human conscience allied to an abject failure of the Church to uphold Christian moral standards.

How are we to understand this failure? It has to do with the ousting of the Incarnation from its central and controlling role in faith and life, and a strange hesitation to apply the truths of Christ and his gospel directly to the moral and social problems of the age. What has occurred is that the attempt to express the relevance of the Christian way of life to society (for example through so-called 'middle axioms') has actually had the effect of opening the Church to the rising tide of secularism. Thus through a sliding conformity of the Church to the world there has taken place a damaging detachment of morality from evangelical belief in God as Creator and Redeemer and its attachment to the political mechanisms of a secular society. Once morality has been uprooted from its foundations in creation and redemption, it becomes subjective and relative, and is assimilated to the hedonistic spirit of the times. That is what happened so drastically in the 'swinging sixties', when our young people, starved of spiritual nourishment, yielded to the appeal of erotic pop music designed to induce and heighten wild emotional states in which moral restraints gave way to rebellion, sexual promiscuity, drunkenness, drugs, suicide and the occult – all of which are still major rock themes. It was in those swinging sixties that some of our Churchmen, in their desire for popular relevance, gave prominence to such slogans as 'make love, not war' and 'charity before chastity', thereby contributing to the breakdown of family structures and the undermining of true human love.

Typical of our times is the confusion of some Churchmen towards the claim that to be 'gay' is a valid alternative way of life. On the one hand this is to give countenance to acts which in Pauline language are 'against nature', but on the other hand it is to lend support to the downward drag of 'naturalism' in which distinctions between right and wrong are rubbed out. Similar ambiguities arise in our relations to the inbuilt harmonies of the created order in which God has placed us, when the natural environment is misused to satisfy selfish human desires. What is desperately needed in this situation is a return to the biblical teaching that moral law and natural law are closely inter-related. They both have their source in the one Word of God by whom all things are made and who became incarnate in Jesus Christ. To uproot the moral law from its ground in creation and redemption means that moral behaviour becomes grounded in what is regarded as human well-being. Then it is taught not because it is true but because it is thought to be helpful to society in producing human and social benefits. Thus Christian morality is made to serve what is imagined to be the greatest happiness of the greatest number – but that is precisely the same utilitarian ethic which all fascist and communist governments have used to justify their totalitarian rule.

There is clearly at work here what the great scientist and social philosopher Michael Polanyi has termed 'moral inversion', the insidious process in which moral passions injected into a utilitarian framework paradoxically become intensified, and are used to justify the fanatical force of a machinery of State violence. It is not something essentially different when political Churchmen today, in their obsession for the social gospel, urge us to accept discredited Marxist economic ideas in order to achieve certain social ends. This is a subtle form of moral inversion when moral motives are attached to the legislative mechanisms of an organized society in order to bring about allegedly humanitarian results. Apart from revealing that these Churchmen have lost faith in the efficacy of the gospel to change the moral behaviour of private and public life, this inversion of moral passion for political ends actually twists moral motives around in an unhelpful way by embodying them in organized structures enforced by secular law. A disguised shift takes place in the call for 'political theology': from 'political = concern for humanitarian needs' to 'political = concern for power-structures enforcing humanitarian ends'. I recall here the repeated insistence of a Ghanaian friend of mine who works among the poor in London that such theology is actually damaging to the poor: they are not loved for Christ's sake or cared for their own sake, but are being manipulated to serve an ideological fantasy. How true H. R. Mackintosh was when he used to say to his students in New College: 'Gentlemen, you will find that it is the people who hand out Gospel tracts who really care for the poor'!

Moral inversion is carried further by political Churchmen and liberal theologians when normal motives like compassion are inverted and are then developed in a social system outside belief in God. Such values are then put forward as the standard by which the teaching of the Holy Scriptures is to be judged, and its message to the poor and oppressed is to be assessed for its success. This means that the absolute centrality of Jesus Christ as the Way, the Truth and the Life, is rejected, for priority is given instead to secular and utilitarian values that are constantly thrust upon us. There is little belief here in the saving grace of the Lord Jesus Christ, and no belief in the power of the gospel to evangelize and transform human culture and society. Is it any wonder that people cease attending the Church on Sundays, for what they hear from the pulpit is what they have already read in the daily and weekly newspapers or can hear at home through radio and television? Is it surprising that the membership of the Church keeps on dwindling away, when people are fed on the dry husks of secular morality, rather than the bread of life and the living water that are offered to us freely in Christ Jesus? Somehow the institutional Church keeps coming between the people and Jesus Christ, obscuring the gospel, but it is Jesus Christ the Saviour of the world in whom they are really interested, not pulpit politicians.

If this appalling state of affairs is to be reversed the Church of Scotland itself must be re-evangelized. It must turn back to its divine source of saving grace in the Lord Jesus Christ and be renewed through the very truths of the gospel upon which it was founded and with which it has been entrusted in its mission to mankind. It must no longer be conformed to this world but be so transformed in its nature and reshaped in its mind that it will be able to discern the will of God and learn to rebuild our family and social structures on the evangelical foundations of Christian morality. Then once again prayers will be offered daily in our homes sanctifying the family structure, and Christian truth will be taught for its own sake in our schools, instead of as just another RE subject presented in such a way as to cancel itself out. Also children and adults alike will learn to read the Bible as a book of divine salvation, and not merely a book of ancient religious history or a work of moral parables. If this could be brought about, our young people, upon whom the future depends, would grow up moulded by the gospel of God's love, and would take their part with joy in the service of Jesus Christ and his Church.

## The Crisis of Community

Throughout the civilized world the patterns of shared human life and culture that have evolved during the last three hundred years are in the process of disintegration, for their foundations have collapsed. In recent visits to China I pointed out to Chinese audiences that Marxism is the social correlate of the old mechanistic explanation of phenomena and its imposition of necessary structures upon nature. That kind of science has gone. A new open-structured science has arisen which is more congenial to the human spirit and which calls for a new social correlate, a free, open-structured society. This is struggling to be born today in Eastern Europe, but that is the kind of society people want in China as well, as the protests in Tiananmen Square made clear. This is also the desire of people in the liberal democracies of the West, for they too have become trapped in obsolete social and economic mechanisms imposed on them by politicians for human welfare. Today we live between the disruption of old ways and the emergence of new ways. It is a difficult period of transition in which moral bankruptcy and social chaos are rampant.

In our country, well-meaning attempts have been made by governments to stem the onset of disintegration and change the patterns of people's lives for the better, but they have manifestly failed. A bitter resentment has set in. This is evident in the jaundiced jealousy of people against achievers, in vandalism of artistic creations or of neighbours' property, but evident also in secondary poverty which (my doctor friends tell me) some people knowingly inflict upon themselves. It is also apparent in the cynical delight that is often taken in depreciation of the beautiful, the pure and the sacred. More alarming in some ways is the desperate concern that men and women in all walks of life today have for what is called their 'image', for it is the symptom of a serious malaise, a frightening loss of identity and a form of schizophrenia in the hidden depths of modern culture. Our society is suffering from a sickness unto death. In earlier times Christianity provided healing for its pathological states, and the Church gave society the inner cohesion it needed. But the situation is now changed: the Church has trivialized its message, lost its Christian distinctiveness and become increasingly secularized, while its ethic is now so merged in popular social life and culture that its standards are hardly distinguishable from the lowest common denominator of civilized behaviour. In fact, what is called 'Christianity' today is a sort of cultural hybrid between Christianity and secular society, so that the Church is infected with the same wasting sickness as the world around it.

If this situation is to be reversed, we must listen again to the voice of the crucified and risen Christ within the framework of the biblical revelation and resolve to be obedient to it. We must recover the gospel as the Apostles proclaimed it, really believe in its transforming power. As the Body of Christ sent by him into the world, the Church must cease to accommodate its life and thought to the framework of secular culture, and seek to bring the undiluted gospel of the crucified and risen Lord to bear directly upon it and transform it. This is an immense missionary task, but a new beginning has now been made by the Kirk in seeking to build ongoing evangelism into every level of its corporate life and activity, although it is sadly lacking in ginger and effectiveness.

What are we to say about a distinctively Christian approach to the crisis of community? Let us focus attention only upon three points.

(1) A clear distinction between community and society, and between Christian individualism and secular individualism, needs to be drawn. Confusion between them distorts the message of the Church and damages its mission. Christianity is concerned with community; politics is concerned with society. In community individuals are personally related to one another through faith in Jesus Christ. In society individuals are legally related to one another through enforced submission to collective ends. The cohesion of the Christian community is spiritual and supernatural; the cohesion of the secular society is legal and compulsory. Of course Christian community and secular society overlap, and there is inevitably tension between them. If Christian community is true to its spiritual nature, it will not allow itself to be domesticated in society, but will seek to evangelize and transform society. The State on its part cannot create the good society any more than it can transform human life, but it can provide the general framework of law within which there may spontaneously arise the community of people who are united to one another through personal commitment to the Lord Jesus and are empowered through the communion of the Holy Spirit. Everything goes wrong whenever the Church relies upon secular power to order human life and legislate community into existence, for that would substitute social mechanisms for the unifying and transforming operation of divine love which alone can provide community with its inner cohesive force.

(2) We must learn again to take original sin seriously: the fact that human beings are separated from God and from one another by deep-seated alienation and self-love. It is sin that separates human beings from God and from each other, so that genuine community cannot arise without our relation to God being set right, and thus our relation to others as well. That is why incarnation and atonement are so central to the gospel. There can be no authentic social existence without divine forgiveness and reconciliation. That is why the central act of our worship of God takes place in Holy Communion where our relations with God and one another are healed. The Grace of the Lord Jesus Christ, the Love of God and the Communion of

the Holy Spirit constitute the trinitarian structure of all Christian faith and life, for we may be joined together as persons in community only on supernatural grounds, as through the Communion of the Spirit we share in the eternal Union and Communion of the Father, the Son and the Holy Spirit. That is what Christian community means, and why any decentralizing of the doctrines of the Incarnation and the Trinity in the life and faith of the Church leads to the crisis of community and the depersonalization of society that we experience today.

All this means that atoning reconciliation with God through the blood of Christ must be brought back into the forefront of the Church's preaching and teaching, and be allowed to have its full impact on our daily life and activity. There is no other way for us to heal the crisis of community, for there is no other remedy for sin. However laudable political measures for the organization of society are, they cannot deal with the root of disorder, but only too often provide evil with the opportunity for a fresh disposition of its forces. As modern terrorism has shown, evil latches on to legal structures and manipulates them as cover for its own wicked ends. That is the point of St. Paul's remark that law can be the strength of sin! The transmutation of society into community may be achieved only in so far as the inner unity of human relations is brought about by the power of the gospel. As John Macmurray insisted: 'Democracy is a religious thing. It cannot be organized into existence. It can only be organized if it already exists.'

(3) The crisis of community is a crisis of mission. The Church is not sent into the world to exist as a comfortable community, but as a community embodying the mission of God's reconciling love to all mankind. Since Jesus Christ is the propitiation not for our sins only but for the sins of the whole world, missionary activity that proclaims Christ as the one mediator between God and man does not arise from any arrogance in the Church. 'There is no other name under heaven given among men whereby we must be saved.' The very existence of the Christian community and its missionary proclamation of Christ as the Saviour of the world belong inseparably together. Where there is no mission, there is no community, for the community arises and continues to spread in being sent by Christ to carry the gospel into the uttermost parts of the earth in evangelical transformation of human life and society. Where there is no engagement in that mission the community severs itself from the very reason and purpose for its existence, and plunges into crisis.

Today, the very essence of the Christian community and its mission are at stake, for the all-important relation between the community and its mission is being undermined. On the one hand, there is an insidious attack upon the relation of the individual to God and with it a destructive trivializing of the personal. As the heavenly Father cares for each sparrow that falls to the ground, and as the shepherd leaves the ninety-nine sheep in the fold to seek and find the one that is lost, so God in Christ calls each one of us to him by name; it is as individuals that we believe and are baptized, and as individual personal beings that we are reconciled to God through Christ and reconciled to one another to form the Christian community. On the other hand, there is an insidious attack upon the relation of mission to the absoluteness and universal Lordship of Jesus Christ. He is the Way, the Truth and the Life; no one comes to the Father except through him. It is the truth of the incarnation that is at stake here, that in Jesus Christ the one and only Lord God has become man, who calls all people to renounce themselves and take up the cross and follow him. Thus at the centre of the Church's faith and its mission is the absolute fact of Christ, before which all other religious commitments and beliefs in our multi-faith and multi-cultural society are relativized. To play down the absoluteness of Jesus Christ in a multi-faith approach is to relativize Christ as the object of faith, to empty the Christian message of its cardinal truth, and trivialize the Christian mission by tearing out of it the all-important ingredient human society needs for inner healing and unification. Yes, it is precisely at this crucial point that the crisis of the Christian community is to be found. And it is over this issue that we will be called to account, when our Lord Jesus Christ comes again to judge the quick and the dead and make all things new: whether we have been faithful to Christ and his gospel.

# Chapter 3

# Must the Kirk Die?

## R.D. Kernohan

*R. D. (Bob) Kernohan is a distinguished journalist, elder of the Kirk and Conservative. He worked in London not, as many had assumed he might, as an MP, but as London editor of the* Glasgow Herald. *He then spent nearly twenty years as editor of the Church of Scotland's magazine* Life and Work, *managing to hold its circulation above 100,000, and became well known as a broadcaster. In recent years he had spoken out against what he sees as the politicization of the Kirk in a leftwards direction and the flight from traditional faith. In this powerfully argued contribution he deals with the plight of the national Church and its future.*

The surest way to secure a new lease of life for any society or institution is to induce an author to pronounce its doom and disappearance. Old-established but struggling political parties are regularly sentenced to death in print after their latest setback. There was even a skilfully false prophet who wrote a book about the 'vanishing Irish'. But it is not so far-fetched to suggest that the Church of Scotland is vanishing, or at least shrinking to an extent that makes it credible to speculate about its disappearance as a significant national institution and international influence. It can only too easily be presented as an enfeebled Church, even a dying one.

Physically and statistically, much of it has vanished. In the immediate aftermath of the 1929 reunion, when the 'Established' Kirk and the United Free Church bridged the once-great divides left by numerous secessions and the great Disruption of 1843, there were about 2,750 congregations. In 1991 there were 1,685, with only 1,258 ministers in parishes. Hundreds of churches have been demolished or linger on in often incongruous new secular uses, not merely in depopulated inner cities but throughout Scotland.

Membership as reckoned by communion rolls – also the Kirk's electoral rolls – has fallen since 1929 (despite an increase in Scottish population) from 1,280,000 adults to 787,000. Sunday school and Bible class numbers have shrunk from 480,000 to 100,000. Membership rose slightly after the end of the Second World War to about

1960 but then went into a steady decline whose full demographic significance is not apparent even yet. For there is not only a shrinking Kirk but an ageing Kirk. In 1931 there were 43,572 new members 'by profession of faith'; in 1990 only 8,483. Kirk baptisms have also fallen, though not nearly so steeply, to under 30 per cent of the children born in Scotland. The fall would be greater if many ministers did not stretch to the legal limit (and sometimes beyond) the official rules about vows, membership and commitment. But the alarming truth is that only about a quarter of those baptized in infancy a generation ago are now 'confirmed' into the Kirk's membership.

In any event, a 'profession of faith' does not necessarily produce an active or even an attending member. There is no evidence that the smaller Kirk is any more committed. Only 56 per cent of enrolled communicants are recorded as having attended at least one communion service in 1990. Although communion attendance records are now less exactly kept, notably where the sacrament is more frequently celebrated or communion cards are no longer issued and counted, there is no doubt that many members 'in good standing' are only occasional attenders.

It is hardly surprising that the public and especially the media perception of the Kirk is of an institution in decline, and often in perplexity. It is also easy to contrast it in the media – whether deliberately or unconsciously is not always clear – with the apparent vigour, coherence and discipline of the Roman Catholic Church in Scotland. In fact the contrast is by no means as clear as sometimes appears, for the Roman Church is increasingly subject to the ills that Protestantism has been heir to. But it does allow inexpert media reporting to suggest that the Roman Catholic Church has overtaken the Kirk in membership, though there is no valid comparison between figures for an adult communicant membership (the usual Protestant basis) and one for baptized 'Catholic population'. This covers an even greater multitude of sins.

However, one roughly accurate estimated statistic – that for church attendance in the 1984 'census' sponsored by the National Bible Society of Scotland – showed how much of the Kirk's influence had vanished as church attendance died away. It found total Kirk all-age attendance on an average Sunday to be about 361,000, only just ahead of the Roman Catholics (who were reported to have had more adults in the pews) though still more than twice the total for all other Protestant Churches put together. It may well be that all these figures – Kirk, RC, and assorted Protestant – have fallen in the years since that census.

Market researchers still expect about two-thirds of Scots to give their religion as Church of Scotland or simply 'Protestant' (usually meaning Presbyterian after a fashion) in any survey, but it is questionable whether such statistics have much meaning and arguable that an ill-defined agnosticism may replace a vague Protestantism as the religious condition of the largest group in the Scottish people.

Yet this national Church, which is now in some ways a minority Church, has been the main Scottish expression of religious feeling for more than four centuries, and the inheritor of the Christian tradition that goes back to Ninian and Columba. It is also a Church which has been the main expression of a Presbyterian tradition which has had an influence in the English-speaking world out of proportion to the size of Scotland. Even in this century George MacLeod, the Baillie brothers, J. S. Stewart, William Barclay and Tom Torrance (the sole surviving Titan) have had an international and inter-denominational influence as Christian theologians or com-municators.

In really great matters the Kirk's affairs have not been badly conducted and its judgements often well-founded. The hopes for national evangelism which were raised by the 1929 Presbyterian reunion have not been fulfilled and the language in which they were expressed – and are still expressed in the Kirk's legal constitution – may now sound embarrassingly triumphalist and self-satisfied. Yet the formula which combines national recognition of religion, the 'establishment' of the historic Scottish Church in national life, and the complete spiritual and practical independence of the Kirk is still often cited and envied beyond the Tweed.

It remains a comprehensive and on the whole a tolerant Church, a house of many theological mansions and considerable liturgical variations. It may, about once in a decade, get unduly excited about ministers and elders who develop doubts about infant baptism and dip into strange waters, sometimes literally, but it remains (as John Buchan eloquently argued in 1929) a bridge between the churches of order and tradition and those of individuality and inspiration. Even when it is divided and controversial it can find the courage of conviction in coming to a decision then closing ranks to accept it: notably when its 1984 General Assembly sustained a remarkable quality of debate and accepted that Grace might let even a murderer proceed to ordination.

And a generation before the Church of England was even ready to face up to the problem, it had crossed the Rubicon and agreed to ordain women to ministry and eldership on the same terms as men. The surprising thing is not that subsequent developments have provoked occasional grumbles from both feminists and fundamen-talists but that the vast majority of liberals and conservatives have worked to make this evolutionary change a success. For it has been a success, despite the 'Motherhood of God' controversy provoked by an untypical Woman's Guild president from the New Left and the later rumbles of discontent from would-be conscientious objectors among ministers of the farthest fringe of the New Right.

Apart from the unaccountable failure of the nominating committee to take the chance – at least twice offered to it – to have the Kirk's pioneer of women's ordination as Moderator, the slow but steady move of women into the ministry has gone well. Outside some very conservative areas in the Highlands and Islands, most members of the Kirk must now be aware from experience or local repute that some women preach, teach and lead their parishes better than many men. And if anything the much faster move of women into the eldership has gone only too well. It is a good thing (given that women are the majority of regular church-goers and active workers in congregations) that women should be ordained in at least equal numbers, but a bad thing if the accelerating speed of the change reflects a failure to find men of equal quality.

This is one of the areas where the failure of the Kirk has not lain in making wrong decisions or avoiding decisions but in an apparent inability to take credit for its virtues and exploit its successes. Another is the inability to get full benefit from the Presbyterian freedom from set liturgies. The style of services, the choice of music, and the language of preaching ought to vary even more than they do to suit the different tastes and social backgrounds of congregations. In theory we should be the most flexible of all Churches in our worship. In practice we are not.

There are at least three other such areas of lost opportunity. If the Kirk grasps their significance it need not die. It will stumble in the dark, humanly frail and fallible, but will be guided by the Light of the World.

The first is the ecumenical Reformed approach to the Lord's Supper.

The second is the Reformed experience of the ruling eldership as an important and practical part of the ministry of the whole people of God, within a system which combines elements of both democracy and authority.

The third is the survival, amid much failure and under intense pressure, of the idea of a national Church as a province of the universal Church, reaching out to everyone, ready to help everyone, and anxious to include as many Christians as possible as well as to co-operate with others.

In none of these areas does the Kirk rise towards what one of its sung paraphrases of Scripture calls 'perfection's sacred height'. Yet it has not only moved decisively in the right direction – sometimes at the Reformation, sometimes in the process of continuing reform – but has opportunities if it thinks clearly and acts boldly to renew its own strength and shape a new influence for good. Sometimes, alas, these opportunities are not taken – as in the half-hearted support the Kirk mustered for Billy Graham's Scottish mission in 1991 or the official indifference towards Tom Torrance's 'Urgent Call' a few years before – but others will come.

To some extent the Kirk has taken the opportunity to show that the Lord's supper, the public and joyful display of God's grace and Christ's welcome, should not be hedged about and fenced off by regulations and restrictions. The invitation at a Church of Scotland communion service is now generally extended not only to those enrolled in the congregation, or visiting from other congregations of the Kirk, but to members of all parts of the universal Church. It is true that a desire to do things 'decently and in order' sometimes breeds an unnecessary fussiness, and there are congregations where communion visitors are not made to feel as welcome as they should be. There is also, in parts of the Highlands and Islands, a restrictive attitude – often stronger among the people themselves than the ministers – which leads large numbers of good Christians to hold back from the Lord's Table as 'unworthy' (as if any of us is worthy!). Finally, there is the Kirk's ability to get itself into a fankle over offering the bread and wine to children. The subject bobs back and forwards among General Assembly, Presbyteries and Kirk sessions, although ill-suited to legal regulation and definition.

But for all that, the Scots Kirk has committed itself to opening up the Lord's Supper rather than restricting it. That ought to be a source of strength and it should help in blowing some fresh air into the stale ecumenical discussions about mechanistic theories of apostolic succession and worries about whether the person presiding at the Lord's Table has been adequately licensed by a proper authority.

The long-term consequences of this new ecumenical approach – which is not confined to Presbyterianism or Scotland – are temporarily obscured by the reappraisal and reconstruction of ecumenical structures (for what these are worth) following the Roman Catholic change of policy about participation. In the early years of the new enlarged ecumenical bodies, few of those who are most involved in them want to take risks. On paper the Roman Church has been given a veto on progress towards inter-communion. In practice the issue will not go away and it will not take many 'troublemakers' to stir things up.

Normally it would not be fair to accuse the Iona Community of being among the troublemakers. It is far too conservative a body, set in its ways, reflecting the ideas of the 1930s as worked out for the society of the 1950s, and too rich in the conventional wisdom of political ideas whose time has passed. But its enthusiasm for forcing the pace on inter-communion needs to be taken seriously. It is reported to have set a target for achieving inter-communion by the end of the century and its leaders are said to hope for the day that the Pope can come to Iona and preside at the Lord's Table there.

I suspect that such plans and hopes may have been inadequately reported, though it is possible that the Iona leaders may have been deliberately restrained in their approach. For what is involved in any move to inter-communion is not a dispensation which an exalted personage gives himself, or others, to preside on some special occasion over a congregation including heretics in an ancient church held in trust for Christendom; the day of glory will have arrived if a visiting Bishop of Rome and his Scottish vassals sit or kneel with the ordinary people of God of all denominations, having heard the Word preached by whatever godly man or woman is appointed for the day and accepting the gifts of bread and wine as they pass around the congregation.

This may seem a very Protestant and Reformed view. But then the Kirk is a very Protestant and Reformed Church, for only in that does it fulfill its obligations to the biblically-based 'universal or catholic Church' of which it is a province. Only in being true to Reformed insights can it express its true catholicity. And in both the politics of ecumenism and its mission to Scotland the most important of these insights is the priesthood of all believers – not just as an abstract doctrine but in the practical deployment of these priests to appropriate callings and ministries in the Church.

The Kirk does not mobilize the full potential of its 46,651 elders, appreciably more numerous than in the days of larger membership. But even suppose a quarter of us are too old to do much good and another quarter wonder if we should have accepted ordination: it remains an extraordinary cadre of diverse sorts and conditions of Christian talents, admirably suited for its primary purposes of sharing in spiritual leadership, the rule of the Church locally and nationally, and the heavy load of pastoral work.

Admittedly, some ruling elders have been conditioned to underestimate their collective importance in the Church. They think of themselves as unskilled pastoral auxiliaries. They leave too much to the teaching elders or ministers, and not just the distinctive ministry of Word and Sacrament which belongs to them. They take too much for granted the clericalism that infests some parts of the Kirk's committee structure.

The most obvious example has been in ecumenical representation and delegations, though even there a token elder with conventional views may go far. But there are less obvious and perhaps more important examples where Kirk committees with a large nominal representation of elders have delegated much of their power of initiative to working groups. Sometimes (as in the left-wing groups set up to pronounce on social policy or encourage inverted racism in education) the 'lay' representation may largely exclude elders, even by drawing in ideologically acceptable people from other churches or none. But in key matters concerning Kirk doctrine and practice the atmosphere is clerical enough to make even a Pope blush.

Take the Panel on Doctrine working party of the late 1980s which wanted the term 'ordination' dropped for elders and used its remit on the 'ministry of the eldership' to come up with a scheme for having elders on fixed-term or short-service commissions. The scheme was so unpopular, both in theory and because of its impracticability in many areas, that not one Presbytery was reported as supporting it. The panel itself later admitted that it was 'doubtful' if it would have got so far had a technicality not prevented the General Assembly rejecting it instantly. This working party on ministry which became so conspicuously unsuccessful a committee of inquiry into the eldership consisted of eight ministers and two others, of whom one was not an elder. The 1991 report on the admission of children to communion, with suggestions about the role of district elders, came from eleven ministers and one other person, presumably an elder. The group of twelve which prepared the Kirk's latest draft for a contemporary statement of faith included nine ministers.

These are extreme, though significant, examples of the way the influence of elders in the Kirk falls far short in practice of what might be suggested both by their numbers and talents and by the way Presbyterians sometimes talk of the extent of elders' participation in their system.

But there are signs of hope. There is a desire among elders to be better trained, and practical encouragement for this has often come from ministers in the Kirk's central administration. There is evidence that it is elders who sustain congregations during vacancies, and modern patterns of Kirk life make vacancies more frequent. There is scope also for elders' leadership in another modern pattern, the one which created large parishes after local church unions or entrusts one minister with the charge of two, three or even four linked congregations, each with its own kirk session.

There has also been a world-wide Reformed reaction – as marked in the Kirk as anywhere – against the World Council of Churches' attempt to force the straitjacket of 'threefold ministry' on all Protestantism, following the design of the 'Baptism, Eucharist and Ministry' report. On no ecumenical matter has there been such a clear reaction from the Kirk (in line with other Reformed Churches) uniting theological liberals and conservatives and those who are normally most forward and most cautious in inter-church relations.

Presbyterians in Scotland and elsewhere recognize the vigorous lay contribution which is often now made in Anglicanism and even Roman Catholicism, sometimes showing a freshness and liveliness we might envy and (for example in the Church of England) bringing an infusion of democracy into traditionally authoritarian systems.

There are far-reaching implications in this for the world Church. The Roman Church's troubles with liberation theology and the occasional batch of feminist nuns are surely only hints of things to come.

What is vital in the Reformed or Presbyterian system, and must belong to the world Church, is the provision for 'lay' people – even if that word is ill-suited to our usage and insight – to share in the rule of the Church, temporal, spiritual and doctrinal in a way which ought to stifle clericalism, guard against priestcraft and liberate the ordained ministry of Word and Sacrament for its true role of preaching, teaching and pastoral leadership.

But is is important to guard against the eldership becoming stale – one reason why Presbyterians should attend carefully to the less developed Anglican and RC provisions for lay participation – and to avoid complacency about democracy in the Kirk's policy. It is sometimes described as 'a democratic Church', but that is somewhere between an inaccuracy and a gross exaggeration. It is a Church with some democratic traditions and important democratic elements in its structures, such as the election of ministers and the supremacy of a widely representative General Assembly.

One part of the revival of the Kirk ought to involve a search for ways to infuse new elements of democracy into its system. I suggest two for a start – one of which is not really new but a recovery from a false start and setback. If these two succeed I can see no reason why more radical reforms might not follow.

The most important body in the Kirk, apart from the annual General Assembly, is now the Assembly Council, a body scarcely ten years old. It settles priorities and has done a reasonable job in countering the self-interest and self-centredness of powerful boards and committees. It suffers from the jealousy of those who fear the creation of an executive board and has lost one of its original assets, direct election of independent-minded members by the General Assembly on a single transferable vote system. The history of the matter exposes some of the limitations of the Kirk's democracy. When those who preferred back-room nomination to free elections for the Assembly Council first tried to undo the innovation that they disliked they were challenged on the spur of the moment in a reasonably competent manner from the Assembly floor (modesty forbids me to be more specific), and lost. When they tried again at another Assembly, differently composed, no one acted in time and the reversion to the traditional system went through unopposed. But it would be no bad thing if what the traditionalists feared were to come to pass: if the Kirk had an executive board representative of different schools of thought and responsive to grass-roots pressures.

If the Kirk really wants to have democratic elements in its policy, why not apply the same system to the principal committee involved in commenting on the national practice of democracy, the Church and Nation Committee? The Church and Nation Committee can be controversial and there are those in the Kirk who dislike its high profile, quite apart from those who simply disagree with the leftish opinions which have predominated in recent years. In fact, the committee would benefit from an even wider remit, taking over all matters where the Church must make representations to government about public policy and leaving the Boards of Education and Social Responsibility to concentrate on administration and internal Church affairs. But even without this desirable extension of the Church and Nation Committee's remit, it needs to be more fully representative of the Church. The obvious way to achieve this is for it too to be directly elected by proportional representation.

Directly elected by whom? In the first instance the answer might have to be (as in the original Assembly Council scheme) by the 1,200 or so members of the General Assembly, but there is no reason why democracy in the Kirk should not range much more widely, perhaps to all members of Presbyteries (an electorate of several thousands) or all elders and ministers (an electorate of nearly 50,000) or even all members of the Church. Why not? The day might even come when all members of the Kirk could join in direct election of the Moderator of the General Assembly. If such suggestions seem far-fetched, those who scorn them need to pause to examine their reasons for keeping democracy at such a distance. The two most common really amount to no more than 'We don't do it that way' and 'We fear the results if we did it differently'.

Against that are an argument of principle – that members are entitled to be involved in what is done in their name – and one of proper expediency: that more participatory democracy might quicken the sometimes sluggish pulse of the Kirk, helping it to sustain its role of National Church in a Scotland very different from that of the Disruption of 1843 or the reunion of 1929. Our century looks like ending with a new enthusiasm for democracy, even in places where its forms are adopted without much sign of its spirit, and a reassertion of nationality within or against larger groupings. The Church of Scotland, with its elements of democracy and its sustenance of nationality, ought to be stronger than it is in this environment. It too often appears a Church of the Past when it has what it needs to be a Church of the Future.

Perhaps that contrast is too glib. The real problem of the National Church (or any Church) is that even in a time of frenetic change, technological revolution, social rootlessness, cultural pluralism and moral confusion it has to worship an eternal God and a Christ the same yesterday, today, and forever. Its conscience, like Luther's has to be captive to the Word of God. If the key to national mission lay in loosening doctrinal formulae, the Unitarians would be sweeping all before them. If it lies in unchanging adherence to confessional

Calvinism and seventeenth-century interpretations of Scripture the Free Presbyterians will need a kirk in every Lowland parish.

There are two additional problems for the Church of Scotland. The first is that the ecumenical temper of the times has made it undesirable in some ways, and unfashionable in even more, to express that profound antipathy to the Roman system which for more than four centuries has been an essential, motivating and unifying part of Scottish Protestant religious experience.

What our forefathers called a blasphemous perversion of God's truth – that some frail and fallible creature can be identified as Christ's special vicar on earth – we are now encouraged to think of as merely a different Christian tradition. In a reaction against outmoded theological diatribes and communal sectarianism – the latter alive and well on both sides but expressed in football grounds more than churches – much of the Kirk has lost both the notion and the insights to say what it means to be Protestant, speaking the truth in love. It might make a new start, and save much pain and misunderstanding later, by emphatically rejecting any notion that the See of Rome can ever exercise any primacy, whether in the present authoritarian system or a new conciliar one, over a united Church of Christ. It might be surprised to see how positive the response would be from Protestants throughout the world, and not least from great numbers of Anglicans.

The second problem is that secular forces have usurped the Reformed Church's role, scarcely challenged for more than two centuries after 1707, as the main guardian and supreme expression of Scottish nationality within the United Kingdom. That role was only tenable while the main part of the Scottish people cared intensely about the matters, spiritual and ecclesiastical, which gave Scotland different religious traditions from England. Many of the emotions which today are associated with political nationalism, even some of those more healthily purged from our system at Murrayfield or Hampden, found expression in earlier times in the fight against State intervention in the Kirk or the determination to assert the Scots presence everywhere in the British Empire, which no self-respecting Scot ever considered an English empire.

As we sing at Murrayfield, 'those days are past now'. When the Kirk now affirms its nationality in public it is usually by trying to cadge a place in essentially secular and often suspiciously socialist political campaigns. This has not been an unpopular position with the Scottish media and much public opinion, especially when Mrs Thatcher was in Downing Street, but popularity of this kind should be low among the Kirk's priorities. Those who flatter the Kirk when it supports them and enlist its co-operation for their secular purposes are often totally indifferent to the things that really matter to the Church and in the Church: Grace, repentance, eschatology and the bid to conduct private lives and social life on the basis of the Ten Commandments and Christ's new commandments. Any link between nationality and revival in the Kirk must emerge from the recovery of the idea of a covenanted nation, not the restoration of political independence or a relapse into socialism.

Must the Kirk die then, or survive only in a geriatric condition or as a remnant isolated from the main course of Scottish life? The answer must partly be an act of faith, as all Christianity must be. The other part must be encouragement to the Church of Scotland to go on doing, and try to do better, the things that are unfashionable and difficult and which often involve undervalued assets.

The most vital single duty of the Kirk is to maintain its national territorial ministry throughout the mainland and islands of Scotland. No church should now be closed or united with another when its congregation wants to carry on. If this means too many churches chasing too few ministers we shall simply have to adjust our pattern of church life for a time to make more use of readers (lay preachers) and elders willing to take a local role in leading services. In the longer run we may have to take a much more practical and positive view of recruitment to the ministry. That is no far-fetched idea. After all we have been turning away more candidates than have been accepted and, while many mature elders and other members have come forward with a 'call' to the ministry after working elsewhere, we have never planned a campaign to ask them to consider the claims of the ministry. If the Kirk really tried it could have 500 more ministers within five years by asking every elder aged between thirty and fifty-five to listen for a possible call.

Any remaining problems of 'union and readjustment' in cities and towns with too many churches should be left to market forces. Further closures, where inevitable, should come when a congregation is too weak to carry on and either accepts the fact or fails to make a convincing case for outside financial aid. Intervention from the centre should come only when a church is needed and it cannot carry on unaided. That is bound to be the situation in remote and scattered areas and some city housing schemes where the Kirk is weak in numbers and local leadership. There are inescapable duties there but they are not the only priorities. Too many 'progressives' in the Kirk want to atone for the alleged alienation of the nineteenth-century proletariat at a time when the most serious immediate problem is the quiet drift away of large sections of the suburban, small-town and rural middle classes. Much of what might be called the Govan and Iona analysis of Scotland's needs is obsolete in a society which has lost so much of its heavy industry. Most Scots no longer live either in slum streets or council houses. The Church's problem is not that it has lost a class but that it is losing a nation.

Some necessary reversals of the policy of planned contraction can be effected by changing church law or administrative practices. But survival and revival also involve changes of style, even changes of heart, though some of these will have legal implications. For example in the present climate of opinion the Church should see signs of grace in any requests for marriage and infant baptism. (And it should not worry too much either if someone baptized in infancy feels the urge to repent and be baptized again.) While no minister should or can be forced to marry or baptize against his conscience, the law of the Church should err on the side of being be too permissive rather than risk being too restrictive.

The Church needs to make the most of residual Protestant folk-religion, the inheritance of the centuries, and to handle its own internal conservative revival in a liberal and tolerant spirit. Those who are still within the Church or in touch with it need a new grounding in the Reformed Christian faith. But they and others must never be turned away or turned off when religious instincts reassert themselves, however vaguely or fitfully. There need not be a 'fundamentalist takeover' but a higher proportion of the diminished Church and of its ministry will come from its conservative evangelical wing.

God works in mysterious ways, but he has performed wonders with churches in Central and Eastern Europe which seemed debilitated and near to death under the pressures of a more ruthless secularism than Scotland has encountered. All churches there were the trustees of social and cultural traditions that communism tried to destroy. They expressed and sustained national history and character, suffering persecution yet benefiting from their role as the only institutions not completely under the totalitarian State's control.

Is our distinctive national religious tradition in Scotland to fade away for want of persecution? Surely not. Probably not.

# Chapter 4

# Funding a Spiritual Health Service

Andrew Herron

*Andrew Herron is the doyen of ecclesiastical lawyers. He qualified in law when he was pressed into the role of tribune of the people as parish minister in Houston which was faced with the unwelcome prospect of a new town, and won his case. He continued to win arguments (usually a canny plea for the status quo spiced with wit and practical wisdom) in the General Assembly which elected him Moderator in 1971. As Presbytery Clerk of Glasgow for a generation his carpet was worn thin with those who came to seek his advice and he oversaw the rebuilding of many churches which had been destroyed by the M8 motorway through the city. The author of several books, he was for twenty-five years editor of the* Kirk Year Book *and writes here of the need to conserve a national Church.*

Few subjects can more quickly arouse debate than the question of funding the National Health Service. That it is good there should be a national service responsible for the physical well-being of every citizen without discrimination and requiring no payment by the recipients – this is now accepted. But it costs money, and where is the money to come from? It is a question to which there is no easy answer, but it is capable of generating much heat.

Considering how comparatively recently the National Health Service was established, it may come as a surprise to learn that in Scotland the concept of a national spiritual health service took shape four centuries ago. For that is what the Kirk which the early Reformers sought to establish in Scotland truly was: a national spiritual health service, an idea far in advance of its time. First it was a service, something laid on for the benefit of all. Secondly, it had to do with people's spiritual fitness, their well-being as persons. Thirdly, it was a national service – the Kirk was not a club which you joined, it was there for you and you took advantage of its services or neglected them as you chose. And it was completely free: there was no charge for membership, no fee for services rendered, no bill at the end of the day.

From its earliest days the Kirk in Scotland has been committed to bringing the benefits of the faith to all the people by the provision of the ordinances of religion in every parish of the land. An ambitious project, surely. How did the Reformers envisage the service would be paid for? The bill would be high, for there was involved the building and maintaining of kirks, schools and manses, as well as the paying of ministers and dominies. Where was the money to come from?

The answer is that they were proposing to put to good use what was still available of the vast wealth amassed by the Roman Catholic Church; as Cromwell had put it, they were going to melt down the Apostles in silver and send them around the country doing good. At the time of the Reformation a great deal of that wealth had been creamed off by a rapacious and impoverished nobility, but the lairds were still under obligation out of the fruits of the land to provide certain sums by way of teinds (or land tax) for the support of the Kirk. In fact, in every parish the landowners (heritors, they were called) were required to build and maintain in good order a church big enough to accommodate two-thirds of the examinable persons (men and women of eighteen and over), to provide a manse with the usual outbuildings, to set apart a glebe where the minister's pony could be grazed, and to pay the minister by way of stipend certain fixed quantities of locally-grown grains.

This last item created some interesting problems. It was known as 'victual stipend' and was carefully specified in terms of so many bolls of barley, so many chalders of meal, and so on. Indeed at one time it may well have been collected in just that form. An Act of 1808 regularized the whole affair by providing machinery for translating from victuals to cash. This lay in creating in every county a court which would have the duty of fixing 'fiars prices'. Few ministers of today have so much as heard this quaint term, but to our fathers of last century it was a matter of urgent concern – so much so that the fiars' prices for each county can still be found set forth in full on the opening pages of early Church of Scotland Year Books.

What are fiars' prices and whence their name? According to The Digest of Church Law by Dr. William Mair the origin of the name is unknown. The thing itself, however, is clear enough. The Act required that some time between 15 February and 3 March in each year in every county in Scotland the sheriff sit with fifteen jurymen, being knowledgeable persons living within the sheriffdom, to hear evidence from proper witnesses as to the prices that had obtained in the area for various commodities, for by this time the last of them had been sold. As a result of this hearing 'fiars were struck' and judgement given before 12 March. Thus the minister, having a list of the various quantities of grain and meal due to him by the various heritors, had now also a fixed price for each of these and was in a position to know how much stipend he was due. His worries might have seemed to be at an end, but not so.

It would appear that not all 'bolls' were of the same size, and the minister of Neilston is heard complaining that one-half of the stipend due to him is paid in Linlithgow bolls and that this has the effect of reducing that half by 6 per cent of the local Renfrewshire boll. Short-changing the Kirk did not perish with Ananias and Sapphira!

A more general complaint arose from the fact that the price struck was for the previous year. Which meant, of course, that it was 12 March before the minister so much as knew how much stipend was due *for the previous year*. And he had still to collect it.

A further complication was that stipend 'vested' twice in the year, at Whit Sunday and Michaelmas (15 May and 29 September), and whoever was incumbent on these dates was entitled to that half. Not only, then, was the year not evenly split into two (as it would have been had Martinmas been taken instead of Michaelmas) but there was this peculiarity that it didn't matter how long you had already been, or how long you were going to stay, you were due the half-year's stipend when it vested. That is to say, if there was a half-year's stipend to get. There is a tale of a prospective widow who insisted on giving the servants a weekend off so there would be no witnesses as to precisely which side of the Michaelmas divide saw her husband's decease.

In addition there was the 'Law of Ann' to be reckoned with. This decreed that the half-year's stipend vesting immediately after the death of a minister went to his widow as her personal property (not as part of his estate). In general terms 'Ann' was fair enough in that the husband had probably gone without stipend for a long period at the beginning of his ministry and the widow was just catching up.

An entertaining tale could be written about how the heritors' obligations in respect of the manse were fulfilled. Many were the cases that went to the courts and there is a deal of case-law about what were the proper requirements.

It was thus that the national spiritual health service was funded.

In a word, through many generations in Scotland the costs of a territorial ministry were met by a tax on the fruits of the earth, those who were free to enjoy the benefits not being expected to make any contribution towards the cost.

In fact, collections were taken at every church service, sometimes by bag or ladle during the service, sometimes by plate at the Kirk door or even at the kirkyard gate, but these were invariably for the poor of the parish and they were, of course, voluntary offerings. For us children of the welfare state it is hard to conceive a situation where no provision was made by the State for poverty of whatever kind or degree. Yet so it was in those early days, and while the help the Kirk could supply was meagre and inadequate it was the only help available. We can claim all along to have been a caring Kirk. The enormous social revolution consequent on the Industrial Revolution made it essential that the State accept the responsibility that had so long lain on the Kirk, but it was still 'parish relief', bearing testimony to its original source.

## The Act of 1925

With very little change things continued in the old parish Church until the fateful year 1925. Around that time, in preparation for the Union of the Churches in 1929, many matters of common concern were being critically looked at, not least that of statutory provision for stipend. The strong 'voluntary' tradition within the United Free Church was highly critical of endowment. To some it smacked of State control. The outcome of this review was the enacting by Parliament of the Church of Scotland (Property and Endowments) Act of 1925, one of the principal effects of which was to change what had been a tax on the fruits of the earth into a standard charge. Stipends were standardized – that is to say, they were fixed at a definite sum for all time coming, and were to be paid *de die in diem*. The standardized figure was to be the average stipend from 1873 to 1922 with an addition of 5 per cent. The change was to take place of necessity at the first vacancy, but provision was made whereby an incumbent could elect to have the change made, and as at that time the standardized figure was marginally better than the other most ministers so chose. A few, however, hung out – the Scottish minister has never been keen on bandwagons – and it is only comparatively recently that the last teind stipend ceased to be paid. Those who hung out did rather well. When the minimum was £450, Neilston, unstandardized, was just short of £2,000.

It all sounded very fine, if not actually advantageous. But it took no account of a phenomenon of little significance at the time but soon to become of terrifying importance – inflation. Before 1925 the teind was nearly sufficient to maintain all the parish ministers in Scotland. Today the entire income from teinds provides a little additional endowment to a few parishes.

In a word, then, so far as the payment of ministers is concerned the old 'funding' is no more.

The Act of 1925 dealt with property as well as endowments and this it did by providing that all heritable property in the form of churches, church halls, manses and glebes passed from the heritors into the absolute possession of the Church, to be held by the General Trustees and to be maintained by the congregations involved. Before the transfer was effected all properties had to be put into a proper state of repair or a sum of money had to be paid over to cover the cost of necessary work outstanding. Thus the Kirk while nominally being enriched was in fact having to assume a vast liability of which in the past it had known nothing. Indeed, it is only in recent days that the magnitude of that financial burden is coming to be recognized.

The responsibility of the heritors in the matter of the erection of churches had become a very sore point indeed. For one thing there had been considerable movement of population thus requiring enlarged churches to be built in what had become populous areas. For another, in the larger towns the number of heritors had increased enormously through allocating strips of land to private houseowners who paid feu-duty and accepted responsibility for teind. This normally would be a trifling sum paid under the head of stipend and was accepted without too much fuss, but when it came to building a new church the financial involvement was of a totally different degree, and difficult cases arose.

When John White went to be minister of Shettleston in 1893 he found the church in a miserable state of disrepair as well as being quite inadequate in the matter of size. He met with violent opposition in his demand for a new church, but finally the new Shettleston Parish Church was built at the expense of the heritors. The last case of the kind was at Cathcart where a similar situation had developed. I can myself vaguely recall seeing a fairly modest protest march of people with banners complaining of their wrongs.

It was surely a haphazard way of meeting the problem of new church building. But there is no doubt the Kirk felt the pinch very acutely when it had to organize its own Church Extension scheme in the 1930s to cope with the needs of the enormous new housing estates sprouting on the fringes of every town and city. Nor can there be any doubt but that the heritors, however unwillingly, erected buildings of a durability that the Kirk itself never contrived to equal.

The spiritual health service has now lost the last vestige of funding from sources outside the Kirk's own membership.

## The Secessions

To console, if not to compensate, them for the considerable financial outlays they had to meet, the heritors until as recently as 1875 enjoyed the right of presenting a minister to fill the charge when vacant. In the early days, grants of lands and money were often made by landowners to set up a cause for the benefit of their tenants and vassals, and it was natural they should retain the right of making appointments to their own benefices. The system seems to have worked perfectly well, even after the Reformation. It was only a right of presentation; once inducted the minister was in full charge of the situation and could not be given instructions or dismissed except by a court of the Church. Indeed, before induction a court of the Church had to approve of his qualifications.

By the time of the Stuarts this matter of presentation was giving great offence and at the time of the Revolution William of Orange was persuaded – against his own better judgement, one feels – to amend the secular constitution so that although strictly speaking patronage was not abolished, the right to appoint passed to the elders and heritors of the parish concerned. All of this was to be dependent on the parish paying the former patron compensation. The degree of interest in the whole affair is reflected in the fact that only two parishes – the two Monklands – paid compensation and obtained the patron's renunciation. In any case in 1712 an Act was passed restoring patronage. It seems pretty certain that a hope of seeing the Stuarts restored was the real motive behind the move; but whatever may have inspired it the Act was passed, and a sorry chapter ensued in the history of the Kirk – years of bitterness, division and strife, two Secessions and a Disruption. Whatever basic differences of creed and outlook may have been the ultimate cause of the conflicts of these years the contestants found in the question of patronage good reason to join issue and good ground on which to fight their battles.

A little to the east of the A9 Motorway as it passes through what used to be the county of Kinross there is at the side of the old road from Queensferry the tiny clachan of Gairney Bridge, consisting of a farm steading and a few cottages. Beside the farm there rises a great obelisk to mark the spot where on 3 December 1733 four ministers of the Kirk, all of them under suspension, met and after much prayer and debate formed themselves into a presbytery which was later to become a Synod – the Associate Synod. Leader of the group was Ebenezer Erskine.

It had all started fairly simply – as great movements generally do – when the Assembly of 1732 passed an Act whereby when the right of presentation passed to the presbytery the choice was to be made by the heritors and elders, the congregation being reserved a right to object. In all the circumstances this seemed if not fair enough at least trivial enough to let pass – but not so to Ebenezer Erskine, minister at Orwell. He happened to be the new Moderator of Synod and took the opportunity when, in that capacity, he preached at the opening of the court to make the most bitter and hostile criticism of what was by now the law of the Kirk. For this he was taken to task and one thing led to another until at the Assembly of 1733 he, along with three others, was suspended from office. These were the four who, along with Ebenezer's brother Ralph, minister at Dumfermline, met at Gairney Bridge that cold December day and formed the Associate Presbytery.

It seems clear they had at that stage no thought of setting up a rival denomination. Rather they saw themselves as a group called of God to lead the Kirk in the true direction – one in which sooner or later it was bound to follow. But for the time being, until the others came to their senses, they had to set themselves apart, not as a competing or dissenting group but as an associate one – hence their name. The last thing on their minds was how they were to progress so far as funding was concerned. For the next seven years they continued to function in their parishes, occupying their manses, collecting their stipends, and from that point of view carrying on 'business as usual'. From the standpoint of the national Kirk, however, such an arrangement could not be allowed to continue indefinitely, so the Assembly of 1740 by a very large majority deposed all five.

Almost in spite of itself the First Secession was now a fact of life.

It was not long before congregations began to be formed of those out of sympathy with the establishment who found an acceptable refuge with the Seceders. The operation of patronage had sown disaffection in parishes where an unpopular presentee was minister; there was in many quarters an upsurge of evangelical fervour for which the local Kirk had little sympathy; and generally there was in the Kirk a widespread feeling of unrest.

An outlet for the discontented had been found in the creation in many parts of the country of 'Praying Societies' that had no allegiance to the Kirk. Things were ripe for change and the emergence of the new church came to many as an answer to prayer. The west had not been represented at Gairney Bridge, yet very soon there came to the Associate Presbytery a petition bearing the signatures of eighty-three persons being members of Praying Societies in and around Glasgow craving to be 'taken under their inspection'. Thus the Associate Presbytery very soon had congregations in Rutherglen, Cadder and New Kilpatrick, shortly to be joined by others from Mearns, Neilston, Kirkintilloch and Old Monkland. The success of the new venture seemed secured. It was indeed a tragedy, therefore, that so early as 1746 the controversy over the interpretation of the Burgess' Oath should not merely have split the new denomination into two bodies – Burghers and Anti-burghers – but that they should have devoted so much of their energies to miscalling and excommunicating one another. (The original purpose of the Oath was a loyalty test to weed out Jacobite sympathisers following the 1745 Rebellion.) Then towards the end of the century the division between those who clung firmly to the old standards and those who believed that a fresh vision of the truth could be vouchsafed – Auld Lichts and New Lichts – split both camps down the middle. So that what had been the First Secession entered the nineteenth century as four separate Churches.

While the Burgher battle was still raging among the Seceders the Second Secession from the Kirk occurred in 1753. Once again the reason was, ostensibly at least, the sore point about the intrusion of an unacceptable presentee. The Parish of Inverkeithing being vacant, the patron made presentation to Andrew Richardson of Broughton, and to this there was strong local opposition (though he was to become a most popular and well-loved minister of the parish). At the time, though, it was claimed that only twenty-two heads of families, one elder and the landed interests were in his favour while 150 heads of families were hostile. The presbytery refused to sustain the call but a higher court upheld it and ordained that induction proceed. It was always difficult in such cases to carry through an induction, the neighbouring ministers being loath to be seen publicly taking sides (the unpopular side at that) in a controversy on their own doorstep. A custom had developed whereby the superior court appointed what came to be called a 'Riding Committee' – a quorum of ministers from outwith the area – to do the needful.

But by 1753 the Kirk had decided it could not side-step the issue any longer. The situation at Inverkeithing having got as far as the Commission of Assembly, that body ordained that on a certain day the presbytery was to meet and carry through the induction, reporting diligence to the Assembly which would by then be in session. Not only so, it was required that the quorum be increased form the customary three to five. On the day following that appointed it was reported to the Assembly that it had been impossible to constitute the presbytery since only three ministers had been present.

Six of the absentees gave in a paper claiming conscience as ground of non-compliance. One of their number, Thomas Gillespie, read a paper on his own account quoting Acts of Assembly dealing with this grievance. It did not avail him. It had all along been understood that an example would be made, so it came as no surprise when it was resolved by fifty-two to four (with 102 abstentions) that he should be the one to suffer. Sentence was accordingly passed with all due solemnity.

A more unlikely leader of a movement of revolt it would have been hard to imagine. His sole reaction to his deposition was to continue to conduct services within the parish first in the open air and then in a barn, until three years later his followers built a church in nearby Dunfermline. In October 1761 Gillespie met, along with Thomas Collier who had come back from England to his native Fife to serve a group of dissenters in Colinsburgh, and Thomas Boston, minister of a meeting-house in Jedburgh, to form the Presbytery of Relief 'for the relief of Christians oppressed in their Christian principles'. The Second Secession was now an accomplished fact.

Though each owed its existence to a common complaint the two Secessions were vastly different in their witness and went their separate ways until 1847 when they united to form the United Presbyterian Church. To some extent the differences may be traced to differences in their leaders: Erskine was self-confident and even spiritually arrogant, Gillespie timid and self-effacing. The First Secession Church was so sure of itself, so thoroughly committed to the Covenants as to be bound to split into sects; the Relief Church had no time for the Covenants, wanted neither part not lot with the civil magistrate, and showed a spirit of tolerance quite foreign to its time in welcoming to the Lord's Table members of other denominations. Gillespie himself never lost his affection for a Kirk that had treated him so harshly, and on his death-bed he urged his congregation to seek readmission to it.

We seem to have wandered very far from our theme of funding, but I think it important to understand the position of United Presbyterianism in regard to this, and I am convinced the history of that body goes far to supply an explanation. I propose that in spite of their serious differences we should for our present purpose treat the two Secessions together under the name of United Presbyterian, for in the matter of funding they were much of a common mind and indeed their general attitude survives to this day in charges of that tradition. I think of four characteristics. First, they drew a very firm and precise line between spiritual and temporal. Secondly, they were proud of their ownership of heritable property. Thirdly, they were inclined to look upon their minister as their employee. And fourthly, they were not at all parish-orientated.

Some part of the explanation for all this lies in the way they began. When these little groups of people gathered together in congregations they must have found they were facing quite terrifying financial problems. The idea that congregations should subscribe in any substantial degree was utterly foreign to the old Kirk, a few coppers in the plate being the standard level of generosity, though even that was sometimes grudged. We read of an Ayrshire congregation appealing to the heritors to have the graveyard walls repaired, complaining of the loss of revenue through gaps in the dyke allowing access to the Kirk without having to pass the elders at the plate. (I thought lang-luggit Ayrshire elders would have been smart enough to alter the siting of the plate!) But this new congregation had to raise from within its own membership the funds needed to build church and manse and to pay stipend. It was of grim necessity that they gave so much thought to their temporal affairs.

They must have looked to the old Kirk for a model of how things should be run. There they had heritors responsible for meeting the bills but who had nothing to do with the life of the congregation. Why then should they not have a body comparable as near as possible who, from a superior position outside the spiritual life of the congregation, could manage their affairs? So the idea of the UP Managers emerged. They were members of the congregation, but under their Preses (chairman) they occupied a very exalted place, taking orders, certainly, from the congregation at the Annual Meeting but not answerable to Kirk Session or superior courts. (I have heard the ingenious argument that since the Kirk Session is the lowest court of the Church it must be inferior to the Managers!)

Some of their number were fairly certain to be the persons in whose name the heritable properties were registered and they took complete control of everything concerned with money, with the solitary exception of the Poor Fund – always the affair of the Kirk Session. I remember a case where the Managers having decided to redecorate the Church, the Kirk Session was invited to make other arrangements for worship on two specified Sundays. On the Saturday evening before the rededication a Manager kindly disposed towards the minister took him into the Church (under cover of darkness) to let him see what had been done. A minister's mind should be on higher things than paint and varnish.

It is symbolic of this sharp division that to this day in former UP charges the tradition is that the minister opens the annual business meeting with prayer and then departs.

This rigid separation of spiritual and temporal is, as we all know, essentially false. The most exalted spiritual exercise has its temporal expression, the most sordid temporal affair has its spiritual implications. The Session resolves, 'It would be good to hold a weeknight service' – clearly a judgement in the spiritual realm. The Managers reply, 'Sorry, we can't afford the heating' – clearly a temporal conclusion. Life cannot be compartmentalized in that kind of way. Even the colour on the church walls can have spiritual undertones!

What of the second matter, the buildings? The congregation had to find money to buy land and build church and manse – a very considerable task involving in the first place the borrowing of money with the subsequent misery of overhanging debt. It is quite enlightening to find Small in his delightful *History of the Congregations of the UP Church* beginning each new ministry by telling of the stipend arrangements and recording the amount of debt still outstanding on the property. He tells too of every major effort to reduce the debt. It is not to be wondered at if they were jealous of their property.

Another factor contributing to the concern over property was the danger of its being lost through internal conflict and division. By and large United Presbyterians tended to be people who, feeling very strongly about certain issues, wanted a Church conforming exactly to their views and not very tolerant of those who thought otherwise. Conscience does not always endear us to our neighbours. Hence the tendency to create division. When some internal strife resulted in the departure of a disaffected member it caused no difficulty, but when a group, perhaps a quite substantial and influential group, hived off there was a real possibility of their claiming the property by arguing that although they were a minority, they were continuing to bear witness to the principles for whose honouring the Church had been erected. And on occasion this view was upheld by the courts, most notably – though much later – in the famous Free Church case finally issued by the Lords in 1904. So that even after the last of the debt had been cleared the UP congregation could never feel too secure in the enjoyment of its buildings.

There are exceptions to every rule and it would seem that not every UP group looked on its investment in property with the same sense of responsibility. A remarkable case occurred in Glasgow. In 1835, Walter Duncan recently inducted as minister of an Anti-burgher congregation in the city was deposed for some fairly minor indiscretion. The charge therefore fell vacant and the majority wanted to waste no time in getting it filled. But there were those admirers of Mr Duncan who felt sure their young minister would shortly have his status restored and they wanted the seat kept warm for his return. The matter went to the presbytery where, naturally, judgement was given for those wanting the vacancy filled. The minority walked out, got themselves recognized as a new congregation, bought a site in nearby Regent Place and erected on it a splendid new church, without, be it said, having paid for it. They then appealed to the Synod to have Mr Duncan restored to office so that they might call him. Their crave was refused. That was bad, but worse was to come. Mr Duncan himself took a hand in things, abandoning the denomination that didn't want him and raising an Independent flag with services in the Trades House, whither his admirers all followed him. So, within ten months the new cause, Regent Place East, found itself without a minister, without a congregation, without funds, and without a future, but with a fine new 1,300-seater church and a fine big bill.

To move to our third characteristic. Plenty of thought and care, and a lot of time, seem to have gone into the choosing of a new minister, and presbyteries spent hours debating between competing calls. Once inducted, however, he would appear in many cases to have had a raw deal, for if he did not happen to commend himself to certain elements in the membership, pressure was brought to bear to expedite his departure. From time to time we read of a minister being told by his flock that it was time he retired, there are instances aplenty of congregations petitioning the presbytery to examine their affairs with a view to having the pastoral tie dissolved.

While presbyteries were not keen to take this step, they often did. Induction was not *ad vitam aut culpam* unless it be seen as culpable not wholly to commend yourself to all your people.

It is said of a Paisley minister that his Kirk Session waited on him to suggest the time had come when he should be thinking of enjoying a well-earned rest and other such euphemistic hints. 'But,' he said, 'I don't need a rest. I am perfectly fit for my work. Has anyone suggested I am not doing my work?' Said one elder a trifle hesitantly, 'Some of the older folk are saying they are not hearing you so well lately' – to which came the unanswerable reply, 'And have they any reason to believe they would hear me any better were I to retire?'

Stipends varied enormously as between one congregation and another, but what must have been far more serious was that stipend stood comparatively low on the priority list and when money was short the payment of stipend due might be delayed for long periods. There would appear to have been the very minimum of central organization in this matter, each congregation being left to manage its own. The first Secession congregation in Glasgow built themselves a very modest meeting-house in Shuttle Street and having called James Fisher, son-in-law of Ebenezer Erskine, promised him a stipend of £100 and a manse. That was in 1739 and represented a very high level of generosity. Some thirty years later the first minister was appointed to the Burgher cause in Pollokshaws, the stipend being £60 'which the Presbytery wished supplemented with a house'. In Largs in 1783 £50 and a free house was on offer while Shotts did considerably better in 1774 with £50 and a house 'and either an additional £5 or as much land as keep a horse and a cow summer and winter'. At Tarbolton in 1777 Presbytery declined to sustain a call unless they were prepared to pay £60 a year and provide a free house.

There is a touching reference in a case where a call had gone to a young minister and though the stipend was of the lowest they promised to fit him out with 'a suit of clothes, a hat, and a pair of boots – and if there was enough over they proposed to whitewash the interior of the meeting house. One hopes there was no skimping on the suit in the interest of the redecoration.

At the other extreme some congregations were able and willing to pay very generous sums by way of stipend. As an admittedly extreme example the second minister of Belhaven in Glasgow was in receipt of £1,000 in 1879, at a time when strenuous efforts were being made to ensure that none would fall below the £200 level.

Along with the individualism that characterized this denomination, there went an almost belligerent voluntaryism in the spirit of which, nearly a century later, one or two congregations of this tradition agreed to enter the Union of 1929 only on receiving a written assurance that never in any time coming would they be required to accept any form of endowment over which the State might seem to have any kind of control.

There was also an acceptance of the principle that the strong were under obligation to assist the weak, though it was as late as 1868 that this found expression in the setting up of the Augmentation Fund under a special committee whose business it was to ingather contributions from those congregations that could afford them and to administer these through a system of supplements to lower-paid ministers so that none had less than £160 per annum.

The last point: United Presbyterian charges were not in any sense parish churches. They were sited in what were deemed to be districts where they might expect to attract members. In so far as specific areas were allocated to them these were catchment areas within which additional members might be sought, they were not areas for the spiritual well-being of which they accepted any responsibility. They did not have a Poor Fund for the poor of the parish; they had a Benevolent Fund for the less well-off in the congregation. They were medical clubs rather than part of a national health service. This is not to say that such congregations were without a missionary consciousness, but that found expression usually in running a 'mission' in what today we should call a deprived area, possibly at a considerable distance from the church itself.

It must never be forgotten that these congregations were dependent for their very existence on attracting enough people of substance and generosity to enable them to pay their bills. Hence the tendency very often for them to be on the move. There was no parish to anchor them and there was both greater need and greater opportunity in new developing areas. As a district deteriorated in its social standing, the possibility of continuing survival diminished and they had to think of pulling up their roots.

Glasgow's congregation of Wellington was begun among the weavers in what was still the village of Anderston by some members disjoined from the Anti-burgher congregation in Duke Street and was to 'serve residents west of Jamaica Street'. Thirty-five years later they moved to a new building in Wellington Street (later the site of the Alhambra Theatre). Then in 1884 the further move was made to University Avenue. An even more interesting case was Cambridge Street established in 1833 to serve the areas of Cowcaddens and Garnethill. In 1861 eleven of their number formed a committee to examine the possibility of moving to Hillhead. It seemed there was promise of considerable support and a fine church was erected in Great Western Road at Kelvin Bridge – Lansdowne. Most of the Cambridge Street people decided to remain *in situ*, but the minister, Dr Eadie, elected to move west. This apparently gave offence to some and one Sunday morning there was found chalked on the Kirk wall this doggerel:

This church is not for the poor and needy
　but for the rich and Dr Eadie,
The rich may come in and take their seat
　but the poor go on to Cambridge Street.

The jibe was really quite unfair: there was no need for the poor to
'go on to Cambridge Street' – they were there already! The fact
that the bulk of the congregation continued the old allegiance was
evidence, surely, of their concern for the poor and needy.

To sum up. The result of the two Secessions was to establish
churches which were essentially congregational in their outlook even
if Presbyterian in their form of government, congregations dedicated
primarily if not exclusively to providing a spiritual health service for
those who were duly enrolled and paid-up members. Of their
method of funding this service it can only be said that, at least until
1868, it was just about as haphazard as it could possibly be.

## The Disruption

The Disruption was in fact a secession but one so wholly different
from those of a century before as to deserve its distinctive title. It
differed in at least three respects. First in how it came about. It did
not spring from chance reaction to Synod sermon or Inverkeithing
induction but was the outcome of many years of drifting apart by
two bodies within the Kirk and had been seen coming for a very
long time. Secondly in its extent. It involved from the first day
nearly half the ministers and people of the Kirk. And thirdly in its
leadership. In Thomas Chalmers it had a leader endowed with the
unusual combination of great vision and remarkable organizing
ability. All three of these elements played their part in making the
Disruption a unique event.

Can two walk together except they be agreed? asked the prophet
Amos. They can for a time, but sooner or later they will split and
go their separate ways. Certainly that was the case in the Kirk of
the early nineteenth century when two competing interests had
appeared, Moderates and Evangelicals. The former owed their name
to the fact that they stood for the conservative element, inclined to
look upon any excess of zeal as an extravagance, while the Evangelicals saw themselves as the progressive party, including in their ranks
most representatives of the growth area of the Kirk, the Chapels of
Ease. It is not surprising that the leaders of the two groups came
from utterly different backgrounds: Andrew Thomson, minister of
the grand new Church of St. George's in the heart of Edinburgh's
New Town which included in its membership many of the most
highly intellectual and cultured people in Scotland; and Thomas
Chalmers, minister of the recently-created charge of St. John's in

Glasgow which probably embraced more poverty, squalor and privation than any comparable area in Scotland – or in Europe for that matter.

As has been said, the battle lines had been shaping for some years, the issue being mainly the sorry old question of patronage, though doctrinal differences were never far away. However, in 1834, the Evangelicals having gained an ascendancy in voting strength in the Assembly, two momentous Acts were passed and the fight was on, though now, nominally at least, a fight between the courts of the Kirk and the courts of the land.

First of all there was the Veto Act. It had all along been accepted that when a man was presented to a living by the patron the presbytery took him on trials to satisfy itself that he was properly qualified. The Veto Act purported to add to the qualifications that he be acceptable to the congregation – after all that was far more important for a successful ministry than a knowledge of Hebrew. To achieve this object they instructed that if the majority of male heads of families disapproved, the presbytery was to reject. In October of that same year Robert Young was presented to the vacant parish of Auchterarder. Out of 330 heads of families 287 turned out to give the thumbs down and the presbytery reacted as instructed. The matter was appealed to the Court of Session where a full court, by eight votes to five, found against the Assembly. The following year the matter went to the Lords who in due course found against the Church, declaring the Veto Act to be illegal. For a second time the case was taken to the Lords with, from the Evangelicals' point of view, an equally unsatisfactory result.

An even more unhappy situation developed at Marnoch where the majority of the presbytery of Strathbogie, feeling bound by the decision of the civil courts, upheld a call and so put themselves in contempt of the Assembly. The possibilities here were quite terrifying. It was not long before the offending ministers were suspended from office, others being appointed to minister in their parishes; against which they went to the Court of Session and had the intruders interdicted. A pathetic interlude if ever there was one, ending with the new minister being inducted by half of the presbytery after the whole of a packed congregation had walked out of the church. An eye-witness recorded: 'We have never before seen a minister ordained who had no single parishioner, no human being of his charge, to wish him god-speed and pray for his well-being.'

That same year, 1834, had also seen the passing of the Chapels Act. The creation of Chapels of Ease had been the Kirk's answer to the population explosion of the Industrial Revolution and they laboured under many constitutional disadvantages. The new Act sought to change all this, the chapels were to have their own Kirk Sessions, parishes were to be delimited for them, their ministers were to have seats in the Church courts. The voices of the Moderates were raised in protest. These changes did not lie within the Church's power to effect, the Church had no power to change the law of the land: it had a duty to obey it. They lost by 152 to 103. In the parish of Stewarton a group of Seceders had returned to the Kirk in 1839 and in terms of the new Act their minister was awarded a seat in presbytery and a parish was being carved out for him. The principal heritor raised an action to prevent this, which was upheld by a full Court of Session, it being declared that the Church had no power at its own hand to erect parishes. The writing on the wall was now legible.

It is generally thought the Evangelicals hoped to secure such an ascendancy in the Assembly as to be able to carry a motion completely severing the Church's connection with the State. But such a proposal could not have been passed at any one Assembly; requiring to go to presbyteries under the Barrier Act, there it would surely have perished. As it was, some of the presbyteries, in view of the Stewarton decision, disenfranchised the chapel ministers when it came to appointing commissioners to the Assembly. As May 1843 approached there was much speculation, much uncertainty, much bitter wrangling. The Assembly was due to meet on 18 May and the Lord High Commissioner, the Marquis of Bute, began the day with a levee in the Palace of Holyroodhouse, whose throne-room was packed to suffocation. Directly opposite him hung a portrait of King William III which in the general jostling had become detached from its moorings and came crashing to the floor. In the hush that followed a voice was heard saying: 'There goes the Revolution Settlement!' As a curtain-raiser it could not have been more dramatic had it been deliberately stage-managed.

The rest of the story is well enough known. The Assembly was met in a packed St. Andrew's Church. As soon as the Lord High Commissioner appeared, Dr Welsh, the Moderator, having said the usual short prayer, went on to say that in view of certain events he must protest against proceeding further. He then read the Protest signed by 203 members, laid it on the table, bowed to the Commissioner, took up his cocked hat, stepped down from the chair and left, followed by Chalmers, Candlish and others in vast numbers. The Disruption had occurred.

I earlier mentioned the magnitude of the task confronting Dr Chalmers in the matter of funding the enterprise. Some four hundred ministers left the Establishment, each one deliberately walking out of a manse – with his wife and children – and detaching himself and them from a stipend. Provision had to be made, and that immediately, for these ministers – all four hundred of them. True, many of the people were behind their ministers, determined that a new and a greater church would be created. But this merely aggravated the problem, for it raised the need for the building of churches, manses and even schools.

The nature and extent of the problem had been very clearly foreseen and Chalmers had had a long time to make his plans. His answer to the stipend problem was that there should be set up a Sustentation Fund whereby the new Church would each year provide by voluntary giving what the endowments might have been expected to yield. The figure he set was £54,000. He himself describes the reception accorded to this proposal as being characterized by 'the listlessness not of indifference alone but of real and positive unbelief'. Yet in fact the income for the first year was over £68,000 and within ten years was topping £100,000.

Out of this fund each minister would receive an equal sum representing the basic stipend, and this could be supplemented by direct grant from the congregation. Thus would it be ensured that none need be in want. This payment, known as the 'equal dividend' began at £120, rose in 1879 to £160 and there remained steady during the remainder of its history. In 1900 when UP and Free united, Augmentation and Sustentation Funds continued for some time to function side by side. Later, however, a Central Fund was inaugurated, regulations being framed such as to make more nearly than ever before a minimum stipend fund. Church buildings began to appear in every corner of the land – five hundred of them in the first two years – usually of the simplest so far as design and materials were concerned, to be replaced by more substantial structures as circumstances allowed. The first was a brick building in Edinburgh to house Candlish's followers. In Glasgow by the close of 1844 no fewer than thirteen new buildings were in occupancy, the first of these a new St. George's in West Regent Street opened six months and one day after the breakaway – you'd be lucky to have your planning application lodged by that time today! With many notable exceptions landowners were not kindly disposed towards the new cause and, particularly in the rural areas, great difficulty was often experienced in securing a site for a church and even more for a manse. But there was a great enthusiasm and generosity was on a quite unprecedented scale, so that parish after parish came to be equipped with its Free Kirk sometimes standing cheek by jowl with its competing Auld Kirk, almost invariably strategically placed in the centre of the village.

Schools raised a further complication. A dominie who had joined the Free Church was unacceptable in a parish school – even assuming he was prepared to teach there – so money was ingathered to build Free Church Schools and then Free Church Normal Colleges to train the teachers and then Free Church Colleges to prepare the ministers. There was also a special Manse Fund. A spending spree with a vengeance.

Lest it be thought that the burst of generosity was inspired by a desire to show the Auld Kirk what could be done, it has to be noted that it was around this time that there was first presented to the Kirk generally the challenge of a vast world outside to which the gospel had yet to be preached. The Reformers had set up a self-contained unit, but the time had come when the Church could no longer look wholly at its own needs, it had to accept its share of responsibility for world evangelism. It is not surprising that a large proportion of those engaged in Foreign Mission activity prior to '43 threw in their lot with the new Church which thus found itself heavily involved in India, Africa, Southern Arabia and elsewhere.

The funding of all this wide and varied activity came quite simply from the givings of the members. No longer was the unconsidered trifle in the plate when you happened to be there a sufficient response. Members were followed up by monthly collectors and the whole business of congregational finance was overhauled in a very big way. The Free Kirk had both a sense of parish belonging and a spirit of mission and there can be no doubt but that its great contribution to the witness of the Kirk in Scotland was that it taught people the joy of giving in the service of their Lord. They believed in an international spiritual health service and were prepared to pay for it out of their own pockets.

## The Future

The years since 1929 have seen many developments in the field of funding within the Kirk. In the early years much effort went into organizing a full minimum stipend system, the last thirty years have seen the co-ordination of the various agencies and full budgeting for their activities; recently we have created a Central Fabric Fund.

Two interesting changes, however, have occurred or are in process of occurring and brief reference may be made to these in closing.

One is the change in the character of stipend. Stipend is properly a living out of which the recipient meets all the expenses incurred in earning it: travelling, postage, telephone, stationery, holidays all traditionally had to be met by the minister out of stipend. No longer is this the case, separate provision being made for all of these. The day will come when someone – HM Inspector of Taxes, who knows – will insist that since ministers are now in receipt of salaries these should no longer be called stipends.

Secondly, I fear the manse is on its way out. This matter is presently the subject of special study and I understand it is being recommended that the present system be retained. For this there is much to be said, but my own impression is that we are performing a kind of King Canute act, forbidding the tide to flow. Today's young couple on the positive side want to secure a slice of the market in property to avoid reaching the end of the road without a roof over their heads, and on the negative side refuse to face the cost of heating seven-apartment houses with eleven-foot high ceilings. The writing is on the wall – on the manse wall.

Straws in the wind, if you will. But they represent two significant symbols of the fact that the Kirk is not just another voluntary organization, it is a unique institution that for many centuries has supplied the people of Scotland with a national spiritual health service. It will be sad to see them go.

# Chapter 5

# Reformed, but Still Reformable?

## Johnston R. McKay

*Johnston R. McKay bears the same name as his late father, also a minister, and has acquired the same reputation for trenchant comment. Bearing a first from Cambridge he ministered at Bellahouston in Glasgow, and Paisley Abbey before joining the BBC Religious Department as a senior radio producer. He is a frequent broadcaster, in regular demand as a preacher and is preparing a book on the state of the contemporary Kirk of which this contribution forms part. It will certainly contain no split infinitives, this being a pet hate of Johnston's, another being the city of Edinburgh in which he works, but he balances this by living on the west coast in Largs.*

There was a time when Scottish Presbyterian preachers, in self-congratulatory mood, liked to hang sermons extolling the strengths of their church on a text from Psalm 48: 'Walk round Zion, count her towers, mark well her bulwarks, consider her palaces, then tell generations to come that God is here.' These preachers would move with effortless ease from the signs of strength which pilgrims were encouraged to observe in Jerusalem – towers, bulwarks and places – to what were seen as signs of strength in the Kirk – an educated ministry, a committed eldership, and a system of church government which was thought to be not only appropriate for the Scottish character but also an effective means of ensuring that the ordinances of religion were brought to every corner of Scotland.

Perhaps today the text for the sermon would be different. Indeed, I would suggest that a more suitable one would be the parable Jesus told about the building of a tower requiring a calculation of its cost, or its twin about a king contemplating battle having to assess the strength of his troops, because these traditional strengths of the Church of Scotland are, today, more apparent than real. Yet the Church continues to rely on them as if they still were effective. So much of the Church's strategy today is based on the assumption that what the ministry, the eldership and presbyteries are *in theory*, they also are *in practice*. But that is an assumption which requires at best to be challenged and at worst to be dismissed.

In the late 1980s when the decline in membership and the strain on its finances forced the Church of Scotland to attempt to put its diverse activities into some order of priority, so that a spending policy could be drawn up, the General Assembly of 1989 affirmed that 'priority must be given to the support, continued training and equipping of the ministry of the whole Church, *beginning with the ministry of Word and Sacrament*' (my italics). The seventeenth-century English divine Richard Baxter once wrote, 'All Churches either rise or fall as the Ministry doth rise and fall', and most church members today would agree with that. They have been encouraged to believe that the Church's traditional pride in its educated ministry has been justified, and anyone who suggests to a vacant congregation that it might not be given permission to call a minister is left in no doubt that this would be to deprive the congregation of someone essential to its well-being and health.

The same General Assembly which affirmed the priority of the ministry of Word and Sacrament also received a report which spoke of the 'central and crucial role' of the eldership within the broader ministry of the Church. But when that report went on to suggest that all was not right with the eldership there was something of an outcry. It was as if the Church at large did not want to hear that the practice did not match the theory. A contributor to a broadcast I produced during Billy Graham's mission to Scotland in 1991 spoke in tones much more acceptable to the Church when he claimed that the Kirk's 47,000 elders were the seedbed out of which Billy Graham's vision of Scotland becoming a 'spiritual superpower' might grow into a reality. And you find a similar attitude to the eldership if you ever suggest that 'team ministries' might be an effective use of the Church's resources, for you will be told very quickly, and with some pride, that Scotland has a team ministry in every parish, involving minister and Kirk Session, and that is where its strength lies.

It is perhaps not surprising to find the ministry and the eldership held up as strengths of the Church of Scotland, but it has raised a few eyebrows to hear presbyteries commended not only as appropriate means of administering the Kirk's affairs, but as a basis for evangelism. Yet, in 1983, the General Assembly instructed its Mission Committee to 'devise' (and the use of that verb was perhaps unconsciously significant since it suggests a certain artificiality of construction) 'a coherent, long-term, Presbytery-centred strategy for the evangelization of Scotland'; out of that has grown a Presbytery Development Process which has placed the responsibility for evangelism with presbyteries up and down the land, assisted by a number of Evangelism Organizers.

All of this tends to remind me of a saying of the late Willie Barclay. He was made a Freeman of Motherwell, which, he used to joke, entitled him to graze his horse on Motherwell Common. Which would be all very well if he had a horse . . . or Motherwell had a Common! It is all very well for the Church to place its confidence in an educated ministry, a committed eldership and a system of evangelically concerned presbyteries so long as the ministry *is* educated, and the eldership *is* committed, and presbyteries *are* evangelically orientated. But if they are not, then the strategy is misplaced because it has been based on theories which are not matched in practice, by appearances which bear little similarity to reality. The king is preparing for battle on the basis of the manuals, and not after a assessment of the troops!

I want to look in turn at the ministry, the eldership and the presbytery because if I am right, it is in mistaking the appearance (or the theory) for the reality (or the facts) that has led the Church of Scotland into false strategies for evangelism and equally false hopes for its success.

The ministry of the Church of Scotland today is not the educated ministry of the past. I am well aware of wisecracks about academic qualifications leading the church 'to die by degrees', and just as aware that anyone who argues for a truly educated ministry is likely to be told that neither Jesus nor those he called to follow him had any formal academic qualifications. But these replies fail to take account of the nature of the society in which the Church has to operate today.

Recently I watched the marketing consultant Dr. Michael Kelly being interviewed on STV's religious magazine programme 'Eikon'. Asked how the Church could more effectively market itself, he pointed out that the traditional sermon was effective in an age when people were accustomed to listening to lectures for an hour or so but was an inappropriate vehicle for communication today – a point which had also been made by the Revd. John Bell at the 1991 General Assembly when he described the heyday of the sermon as also the heyday of the lectures his grandfather used to queue to attend in the Co-operative Hall in Kilmarnock. More substantially, Dr. Kelly went on to advise that sermons must not only be shorter but must carry intellectual credibility in an increasingly educated society.

The *Glasgow Herald*'s columnist Julie Davidson, reflecting on Billy Graham's mission to Scotland in 1991, somewhat wistfully wrote:

> When he [Billy Graham] says that the way to fill the Scottish churches is to preach the Gospel simply, as it was first preached to Christ's followers, I fear that last two thousand years have passed him by. We are not priest-ridden Palestinian farmers and fishermen, occupying a world where the capacity for action was as limited as the range of moral choices. We are creatures of a universe infinitely more complex . . . I have never walked into a great cathedral without tears in my eyes. The baptismal doxology makes me choke over the christenings of strange babies. I've lit candles

and said prayers in churches all over Europe because the idea moves me, although I'm not a Roman Catholic. At a less emotional level, the English of the Authorised Version [of the Bible] satisfies a love of language more effectively than any other prose. I believe, too, that the principles of the New Testament can't be bettered. Like most people I feel a big, rough, incoherent desire to believe in its message of resurrection and redemption. But once away from the big religious occasion it all seems like a blessedly beautiful fairy tale.

Unlike Billy Graham, and those who brought him back to Scotland in 1991, I do not believe the flight from the churches has occurred because of a failure to preach the simple gospel. I believe it has occurred because ministers have failed to speak to those like Julie Davidson, intelligent, well-educated, sympathetic, questioning people whose searchings need to be taken seriously, but who are not understood by a ministry which is ill-prepared to meet them, and increasingly unwilling to attempt to do so.

I will deal first with what I perceive as an increasing unwillingness on the part of ministers to respond effectively to the searching inquiries of many today. Over the past twenty years there has been a considerable increase in conservative evangelical/fundamentalist candidates for the ministry. Now most divinity students begin their studies with a fairly conservative outlook, but in the past they have been sufficiently open to allow their theological education to mould their outlook. It is this which has changed. The tendency today is for many divinity students to begin their studies already convinced of what is the right attitude to the Bible, and what are the fundamentals of the Christian faith, and how these fundamentals may be expressed, and they carry their certainties through their theological training and into the ministry. Those who themselves have no doubts are unlikely to respond sympathetically to others who do, and in this connection I found the most frightening statistic to be revealed by a *Scotland on Sunday* survey into those attending the 1991 General Assembly to be the one which revealed that over 97 per cent admitted to no doubts about the existence of God.

However, the risk to the Church's communication posed by the increase in conservative evangelical ministers isn't simply confined to their lack of sympathy for the growing number of people who cannot share their certainty. It is in what they believe church membership to involve. I recall hearing a speaker at a General Assembly claim that even although the membership of the Church of Scotland had (then) declined to 800,000, that meant, nevertheless, that the Church of Scotland had 800,000 evangelists. In making that claim he betrayed that he believed membership of the Church involved a commitment to evangelical zeal, to sharing faith with others, and to attempting them to embrace the Christian faith. That is exactly what the conservative evangelical will expect of a church member: cast-iron commitment to a sure and certain faith, because that is exactly what the conservative evangelical's own commitment is like. But for many, I would want to argue for most, church members today faith is something they are searching for, unsure about, questioning all the time and certainly hesitant about conveying to anyone else. And in this, I believe church members are being true to the nature of faith, which is always tentative, open to doubt and unlikely to be expressed in the sort of dogmatic propositions beloved of conservative evangelicals. Those who see church membership in terms of an ability to sign on the dotted line at the foot of a series of doctrinal statements will recruit members willing to do so. But they will never attract those who regard faith as a permanently uncertain journey, and refuse to be made to feel guilty because they will not admit they have arrived at the destination.

Those of a conservative evangelical outlook, increasingly dominating the ministry of the Church of Scotland today, are unlikely to provide a form of worship which recognizes the reality of people's attitudes to faith, and so people who are prepared to search will simply stay away. As a former Moderator, Professor Robert Davidson, has written:

> There will always be those who, in an age of increasing perplexity, seek refuge in voices in church or in society who demand a total commitment which refuses to leave any space for questioning or doubt. But there ought to be a place within the church for those who bring their questions with them into commitment and seek within the community of faith to pursue their search for meaning, and equally a place for those who are not sure that they know what commitment means.

These are wise words, but the ministry of the Church of Scotland is increasingly unwilling to recognize that if it does not address precisely the people whom Professor Davidson describes, the Church of Scotland will die. And it will deserve to do so.

However, as well as this unwillingness to accept that the uncommitted searcher has a place within the Church, there is also an inability on the part of ministers adequately to address the genuine questions which are posed by people today, because they are no longer equipped to do so.

Writing only forty years ago about the average training for the ministry, the late G. D. Henderson is describing a world that has long since gone.

> Students have the usual three or four years of study in the Faculty of Arts, and thereafter three sessions of theological instruction, the subjects including Philosophy, History and Psychology of Religion, Dogmatics and History of Dogma, Christian Ethics, Church History, New Testament Language, Literature and Theology, Old Testament, and Practical Theology (covering a wide range of varied training).
> Each student is also attached to some congregation for initiation into

pastoral duties and problems. The spiritual life of students is fostered by regular College Prayers, Retreats, Conferences and other ordinary means; and all students are throughout their Divinity Course under the supervision of their respective Presbyteries and the Church's Committee on Education for the Ministry . . . A few years in a Theological College will not indeed provide all that might be wanted, but it is difficult to be satisfied that without a well-ordered and extended course the ordinary candidate can be directed as he ought towards study and thought, provided with essential tools and shown their use, initiated into method, and can have interest awakened, possibilities suggested and resolves stimulated.

Since the 1950s the training the Church expects from its future ministers has drastically changed. The day when a student took a degree in Arts or Science before proceeding to study theology has virtually gone. Those accepted for even a degree course in theology (as distinct from the less demanding licentiate in theology) are decreasing. And what is expected of either candidates for a divinity degree or a licentiate in theology no longer covers the width of subjects which traditionally the Church expected its ministers to have studied. All of this is partly the result of an attempt to provide courses which are thought to be more appropriate for the increasing number of candidates for the ministry who are older, and who have spent some years in what used to be called 'secular employment', partly it is caused by a desire to make the demands easier to meet, and partly by pressure from the universities to accept candidates who, though less well qualified, nevertheless enhance the university's income. Whatever the cause, the result of the lowering of educational standards for the ministry has been, I believe, a disaster for the Church.

Of course you do not need a university degree to bring comfort to a housebound old person. A knowledge of church history will not make you a better pastor. An understanding of New Testament language and literature will not teach you how to bury a six-week-old baby. A grasp of theology is of very little use when you are confronted by a young widow. But until fairly recently the Church has believed that a broad theological education is more likely to produce a better minister, and one more capable of interpreting his or her experience, than the absence of it.

However, that is not the point. Actually, I believe that ministers are very good, despite the lowering of their educational standards, at providing pastoral support for people in need. But pastoral sensitivity, essential as it is, will not also communicate the Christian faith to those whose rejection of it poses the most serious threat to the Church today: the Julie Davidsons of this world who, if they are not addressed on their intellectual wavelength, will not be addressed at all. Making the support for the ministry of Word and Sacraments a priority for the Church today will fail as a strategy if that ministry has not been equipped to cope with the primary task of the Church today, which in my view is to attract first the attention and then the support of those on the fringes of faith.

You could undertake an interesting exercise, matching the statistics of decline in the Church of Scotland's membership to the dilution of the standards expected to be achieved by its ministers, just as you could similarly compare the drop in the Kirk's numerical strength to a corresponding increase in the number of its elders. Cause and effect? Hardly, but perhaps there is a connection to be drawn if the Church has indeed based part of its strategy on what elders in theory are meant to do while ignoring the failure of the eldership in practice. And I suspect this has been the case.

It is probably not accurate to keep saying that the Church of Scotland loses members. Its congregations do. Members rarely lapse from the Church of Scotland but they do drift away from a particular congregation, and when that happens it is a failure of the Church's link with its members. By and large, and certainly since the decline of the traditional pattern of the minister visiting the congregation systematically, that link has been the elder, each member being allocated an elder whose pastoral responsibility the member is. In theory, of course, there should be no need for a minister systematically to visit the congregation. That is the elder's primary responsibility, bringing to light, as need arises, pastoral concerns which require the minister's attention. But the theory breaks down in practice.

The report on the eldership quoted earlier accurately, I believe, describes the situation:

> Alongside the tremendous service being rendered by the dedicated, we have to acknowledge the negative witness of some among the elders who have long since lost the vision which inspired them to be ordained in the first place, and who would never dream of attending a training course even though they perhaps need it most of all. There are too many Kirk Sessions embarrassed by elders who seldom attend meetings and who carry out their duties only in a desultory way; too many Church members who feel more of a bond with the magazine distributor than with the elder whom they seldom see; too many elders who are no longer finding fulfilment in the job they were ordained to do twenty-five years ago, and whose sense of guilt inhibits them from appearing at Church at all. There exists, it is true, legislation to dismiss elders who absent themselves over a period of time; but it hardly reflects the spirit in which most Kirk Sessions now operate and . . . it takes no account of those who have chalked up the minimum legal requirement and no more.

Some people drift away from congregations because of disagreements with the minister, or a dislike of changes made in the order of service, or a quarrel in the Women's Guild. But most, I suspect, drift away because of lack of regular pastoral contact. I have heard ministers frequently say that they cannot maintain contact with a large congregation, and in any case do not believe they should be expected to do so because 'that is the elders' job'. But what sort of strategy is it that insists on the importance of regular pastoral contact but then consigns the responsibility for it to a group of people known not to be fulfilling their responsibility! Yet that is what is happening in many congregations. Again, the theory and the practice fail to match.

The theory breaks down at other points as well. It claims to save the Church of Scotland from clericalism, and ministers from expectations of omnicompetence by giving to the Kirk Session responsibility for the spiritual oversight of the parish and the organization of the congregation. But in practice, ministers are full-time and elders are busy people. The Church tends to absorb the minister's complete attention; it claims the elders' spare time, and the sensitive minister is all too aware of the other demands made on elders outside the Church. This tends in practice to mean that the minister undertakes more and more of what the theory would say was the Kirk Session's responsibility, not because of any power-complex or workaholism but because, to put it bluntly. 'if the minister doesn't do it, nobody will'. But there is a limit to what ministers can physically undertake, and so inevitably things are left undone which ought to be done.

When, some years ago, the idea was mooted that elders might be ordained not (as at present) for life but for a fixed term of service, the overwhelming response to the proposal was that there should be no change. A fixed term of service might remove some of the problems caused by commitment diminishing while responsibility remains. But the problem of the eldership goes far deeper than the length of time it is undertaken for. It lies in the weight of expectation which four centuries of Presbyterian tradition in Scotland have given to it, an expectation which is seldom fulfilled today, but which still dominates the Kirk's ecclesiastical and missionary strategy. Unless there is a fresh, realistic assessment of the eldership, and a theory of its place developed to match the function it presently meets within the Church of Scotland, the problems it causes will continue to outweigh the usefulness it serves.

In his book *Minority Report*, Dr Andrew Herron writes: 'Evangelism is something to be effected by minister, elder and people in the context of the life of a parish. I think it is important we should say so loudly, clearly and persistently, rather than convey the impression that evangelism is primarily a piece of Presbytery business.' He is commenting on the Church of Scotland's strategy for the evangelization of Scotland, which, the General Assembly instructed should be (in Dr Herron's words): 'Presbytery centred, which is to say that although there was to be a national policy, the responsibility and authority for its implementation would lie squarely at the door of the Presbytery, thus at once providing freedom for local initiatives and allowing no excuse for local *laissez-faire*.'

One can understand why those wanting to have the Church devise a system of evangelism should light on the Presbytery as the ideal agent to promote it. There are around 1,400 parishes in the Church of Scotland, each of the Kirk Sessions accountable to a presbytery for the discharge of its duties. Leaving Kirk Sessions responsible (without providing for accountability for evangelism) clearly would result in little being done, or at least anything which was done being undertaken only by those Kirk Sessions consumed with evangelical zeal. So where better to place responsibility and accountability than with the local presbytery since 'it directly super-intends not only Kirk Sessions but the whole ecclesiastical activity within its bounds'. In theory, the plan should work, but again, theory and practice don't always match each other.

Whatever their origin in Scotland (and there is good evidence to suggest that presbyteries grew out of regular meetings of ministers for prayer and Bible study), they have developed in the Church as judicial and administrative institutions. Their agendas are packed with cases of vacant congregations whose future has to be decided, of all calls to ministers to parishes within the bounds and the trans-lation of ministers to parishes outside the bounds, with the dis-cussions of matters remitted to presbyteries by the General Assembly, with reports from committees mirroring the Boards of the General Assembly, and with quinquennial reports on the life of congregations within the presbytery. The idea that such a body is capable (to say nothing of being willing) to undertake responsibility for evangelism would be laughable if it weren't tragic. Anyone who has tried to persuade a presbytery to undertake any function beyond the judicial or administrative knows that the plan will perish on the inability of a body conceived as having important but limited func-tions to undertake anything beyond these. It is akin to expecting an elephant to run like a gazelle simply because both have four legs and a head to expect a presbytery to become an agent of evangelism purely because it has a specific responsibility for oversight of the parishes within its bounds.

Presbyteries are composed of a minister and an elder from each parish, along with retired ministers and an equal number of elders, plus teachers of religion, members of the Church's diaconate, etc. Ministers can be assumed to have more than a passing interest in evangelism, but those elders who are elected to presbytery seldom come from the ranks of the young. I am not for a moment suggesting that there is an age limit on evangelical zeal, but a glance at the composition of the average presbytery is enough to indicate how risible the idea is that it could become an agent of evangelism.

Presbyteries have an important function to perform, but I suspect even their performance of their limited functions will be diminished if it is assumed they can take on roles for which they are clearly not designed simply because their geographical spread makes them a convenient body on which to place responsibility for evangelism. The strategy, again, will fail because the imagined resources do not match the reality.

Behind all I have said there is an implicit assumption that neither ministry nor eldership nor presbytery is capable of changing in order to meet the needs of the present frightening situation, and yet, does the Church of Scotland not pride itself in being a church *of the reformation, reformata sed semper reformanda,* reformed yet always requiring further reformation? Yes indeed, but here again is the ultimate divergence of theory and practice. While insisting on the need for constant change, the Church of Scotland has become so inherently conservative that any effective change is impossible.

That is a claim which will require justification, for if it is true it inescapably consigns the Church of Scotland to eventual oblivion for (as Andrew Herron himself has pawkily pointed out) 'death is simply the word we use for a failure to adapt to changing circumstances'.

# Chapter 6

# Looking to the Future

William Still

*William Still is the patriarchal figure for conservative evangelicals within the Kirk and the seminal influence behind the Crieff Brotherhood, an invited gathering which assembles every year at the Crieff Hydro. The ministers of those (three) congregations which produce most candidates for the ministry were in turn brought into the ministry partly by his influence. His parish of Gilcomston South in Aberdeen's city centre has been a showcase for biblical expository preaching, and in this reprinted address to the Crieff Brotherhood he argues that it will prove to be the Kirk's salvation in a time of deep recession. While others have taken a more combative line, William Still commands a wide respect for his theology which owes much to Calvin.*

'Where are we then? And where are we going?' Any real act of faith, while it is prepared to take into account all human and demonic factors opposed to its stand, is never daunted by any of them, because it sees the divine Catalyst himself as capable of overturning every flagrant opposition to his will; and, as history proves, creative faith, as a gift of God, often sees its substance realized in a remarkably short space of time, for it laughs at impossibilities, and cries, 'It shall be done!' because, as the earlier lines of that verse state, it looks to the divine promise 'and looks to it, alone.' It does not need to look to anything else: all the obstacles in the world may be ignored. After the union of the churches in 1929, and despite optimism then, the United Church had so little hold on biblical theology that its influence on itself, and on the nation, was bound to wane. Due, largely, to the rising tide of Christian conviction in university Christian Unions, and with the backing of a new race of conservative scholars and their writings (G. T. Manley, Alan Stibbs, Douglas Johnson, Lloyd Jones, F. F. Bruce and others during the period 1930–45, a foundation was secretly laid which made it possible for some of us to get going in our largely moribund denomination, despite the seeming hopelessness of making any impact upon it. We were enabled, by the grace of God, to gain at least a foothold, for what has turned out to be something far more reformed than our immediate forefathers ever knew, and which is represented by many here today.

What happened when Bill Fitch came to Springburnhill Parish Church in 1944 fron Newmilns (the home church of Tom Allan) was perhaps more significant than Bill ever knew. For Springburnhill was not only a formative influence on me but on other leading members of our Brotherhood – the Philips, Eric Alexander, and later also, the major influence of Eric Wright. How many ministers and missionaries, women as well as men, are in the Lord's work and serving God in professional worlds today, due to this one man's influence? So what happened in far-off 1944–5 has turned out to be more significant than any of us ever dreamed.

All this was the raw material – some of it very raw – of the beginnings of this movement which is represented by our Crieff Brotherhood; but its rise (and I want to put stress on this, to the Glory of God) was humanly unpremeditated. It was spontaneous; surprising – except that, in our believing naivety, we 'bashed on', regardless of all the titters, giggles and mordantly caustic comments of worldly-wise ecclesiastics around us. (There are still a few relics of it!) I remember my professor launching a devastating attack on me in Presbytery because I had mentioned hell. He warned the Presbytery to ignore, absolutely, the ravings of this man. I think of so many of our opposers who despised us then – all are dead and gone, and our cause is slowly, but steadily, growing.

Of course, we are still a minority, as our voting at this year's Assembly sadly proved. But don't (like our critics in the other conservative denominations) look at the forest of hands in the Assembly voting for ungodly things; don't look enough to blind your eyes to the growing number of trees in the forest – men who are establishing living churches in the midst of dung-heaps of moderatism in which others, sweetly rotting in their social clubs of polite religiosity, earnestly strive (even to nervous breakdowns) to give their churches credence; desperately trying to boost flagging financial resources with chrysanthemum teas, bring-and-buy efforts and jumble sales. For that Church (if you can call it a Church) is dying on its feet, and is doing so so fast (with multiple economic recessions and modern technology helping, rendering masses of men redundant) that these factors are hastening the time when even prestigious congregations will become little more than mere museums because they have lost (some of them) two, if not three generations of their own youth; and although the old people hold on, and will piously seek to help these places by their legacies when they die, that won't be enough to keep them open for ever. No members, elders or ministers, to say nothing of missionaries, ever emanate from their precincts, and they will all soon have to close their doors unless a new liberal, charismatic figure, like George MacLeod, arises, to make far greater

impact upon the Church than the Iona Community has ever succeeded in doing.

Whereas we are growing, and the Lord is drafting into our ranks,
from all sorts of places and other professions at home and abroad,
a quality of men who know what they believe, and are determined
to process it into the minds and hearts of their people, by means of
the total revelation of God as found in the Scriptures. And all this
with a view to making such vital impact, in time, please God, upon,
first, the Church, and then the nation, as has not been seen in
Scotland since the Reformation.

You need to read closely James Philip's article in *Pulpit and People*
to see what a remarkable thing this systematic biblical expository
ministry is; and although, as Nigel Cameron says in his article in
that book, there are other ways of ministering the whole Word of
God than that, I would like to think that he thinks that this one is
the best possible. Someone was saying the other day, that the discipline alone of facing a passage of Scripture, as the appointment for
the next Lord's Day – a passage, possibly, which one would rather
not tackle – has prospects of character-building potential for a
preacher which will give a resolute ruggedness to his ministry, and
which is bound to produce, as he proceeds through an intelligent,
discriminate selection of books of both Testaments (each portion of
each Testament dealing with successive stages of his congregation's
progress), abundant fruit in the lives of those who respond to it.
And it is from such discipline that the future ministry of our Church
may be expected to rise.

One of the richest fruits of such biblical ministry is the production
of ministers (although Christian school teachers run it a good
second), and many a man is not long in his charge before he sees one
or two or more young men who, quite early, whether he remarks on
it or not, seem destined to make their mark on the ministry of the
Church. There is not the slightest doubt that where this sort of
ministry has been plied and pursued with faithful vigour and intelligent discrimination, the fruits are relatively the same – men and
money: the very things the Establishment is dying for want of.

Now I know that some of you, in your present situations, may
see a great deal of this as either sheer opinionatedness, or prejudice,
or as an idealized counsel of perfection, not at all related to your
present incumbencies. And I know that if I were again in a situation
like yours, I would modify my tactics, and become involved in a
great many of the things which are absolutely necessary for, say, a
housing-estate church. Well, read the first volume of our history
and see what we did at the beginning! But I don't see why the
simple, radical principles evolved in those earlier days by the hand
of God should be any less regarded in such situations because
working towards them must be more protracted, complex and

longer-term. I think it is very wrong of people who are in situations vastly different from those of us with our established conservative congregations to think that the principles I outline do not apply to them. It is the long-term application of these principles which needs to be envisaged. I am now seeing the fruits of forty-one years of effort. And how men in such situations imagine that people in established ministries are critical of them, because they find themselves in the infancy of a work, I cannot imagine. There was here, last year, just a little bit of tension between those in church extension charges and those in other situations, which I think was quite unnecessary, because the fact that we may be all at different stages in the development of the general outworking of biblical ministries is not to say that we must be at loggerheads with each other. Indeed, I count it one of my precious privileges to have the deepest and most personal interest in all these ministries in most difficult situations, and I have often to cry to some of you men in these situations to supply me with fuel for prayer, so that we in Aberdeen may play our full part in seeing you build the kind of churches that surely you, and we, are keen to see established all over our land, with their undoubted outreach to our nation, and, please God, to the world.

In my article in *Life and Work* on the state of the Church, Bob Kernohan raised with me what he called 'minor points' about survival churches, such as in Jerusalem in the early centuries; and then, in the article on 'What is the Church?' which he commissioned and which also appeared in *Life and Work*, he raised the question of the survival of the Church in China during the Cultural Revolution. I attributed its survival to such groups as 'The Little Flock', whereas he thought more emphasis should be put on the survival of the official 'Three Self Movement' Church, not withstanding its co-operation with the communist regime. He also questioned my extreme phrase about the complete lack of congregational structures in Soviet Russia, and in China, when the official churches had structures imposed upon them by the State to control them. I think he was trying to save me from unnecessary criticism from other quarters!

Some of you might raise the same points, since you may think I am apt to be too extreme on the matter of simplifying congregational or other structures. My answer to that would be, that neither in the old Soviet Union nor in China would the official Church ever have led to the reviving of the vital Christianity in these lands which we hear of and read so much about today. I am not saying that there can be no spiritual life where a cumbersome or archaic structure is allowed to survive, for political purposes, for there can be a Church within the church and often is, not least in Scotland today; but surely, even in those far-off situations it is a vital spark, in the person of, say, an orthodox priest like Yakunin, or Capuchio in

Romania, or an unofficial leader like Georgi Vins, or the brave Gospel singer, Valery Barinov, who is the source of inspiration and of conversions. And that has come about only because these men concentrated narrowly on the one thing needful: sitting at Jesus' feet with their Bibles in their hands, and living out the simplest and most radical pattern of life and ministry. And I think that the pattern of expository biblical ministry – which most, if not all, of you here have inherited and which some of you may have fallen into without questioning, or perhaps ever asking how it arose and through whom – becomes such a full-time occupation, even in a church extension situation (although in that one cannot give one's full time to it), that one would be bound in the end to give it more and more time, whatever the complexity of one's congregational situation and the demands of one's parish.

There is a paradox here. Some of you would never dream of enquiring into this, or even attending a service in any of the long-established congregations; or, even if you did, would you think of attending the power-house of prayer there, which is the key to the whole situation. I wonder how few Crieff men have ever experienced our prayer meeting. He's a strange captain of a ship who doesn't want to see the engine-room! Some of you may think that we have run into a cul-de-sac, and have turned Gilcomston, for example, into a narrow little enclave which does nothing but read the Bible and pray. But then, it is that which has produced this, and which has produced extensions of this ministry, not only throughout the land, but in Northern Ireland and the United States, and in Australia and elsewhere. The Word says that the 'broad road leads to destruction', but the so-called narrow way leads to, What? – eternal life, and that is not narrow! If ever I could be convinced that concentration leads to expansion and that quality produces quantity by the outreach (for example) of our small, provincial congregation, it is now. And I think that what I advocate, as an ultimate aim for all of us, is of the essence, both concerning the survival and the revival of the Church in the future. I believe it is elemental, and always has been, to the perpetuation of Christ's Church in the world.

Take the comparative situations in Athens and Corinth. I don't agree that Paul was misguided in what he said at Athens; but Paul's messsage at Corinth was, 'We preach nothing but Christ crucified'; and the Church at Corinth – perhaps the most unsavoury of all the churches with its divisions and its vice – survived. Whereas there is no letter, extant, to any Church in Athens, if there ever was a Church there in that day. But Christ, crucified and risen, takes in the whole of the Scriptures, and if the Church at Corinth survived because the whole Word of God was given them through that text, then that to my mind is an argument for concentration.

What puts many men off this concentration – I don't think we should concentrate to the exclusion of all else, but it ought to be our first priority in thought and action – is that they despise 'the day of small things'. I have often told the story of two ladies from Canada who came to our church one Sunday morning, and as the rather sparse congregation gathered, nothing like a full church, they whispered, 'Can this be the place we were advised to come to?' They, themselves, came from a huge, overflowing church. But they sat; and as the service proceeded, they thought that perhaps it was! I'm sure that the concentration upon feeding the hungry in a congregation, even if there are only one or two hungry souls in it, is the most vital thing that can be done; far more important than the necessary evangelistic preaching, which will undoubtedly be a major preoccupation in an unevangelized situation.

They talk a lot these days about growth, church growth; but growth must come from within. It cannot come from nothing. You cannot have growth where there is nothing to grow. Growth must begin with seed, and the seed is the Word of God; and beyond the sowing of the seed there is the necessity of feeding the germinating seed with nourishment – watering it by prayer. And the seed and its nourishment (this is where that metaphor breaks down) are the same. It is the same Word which evangelizes, and feeds souls.

Now some of you may think that souls will generally only be converted through evangelistic sermons. That is a total travesty of the truth. If the whole of the Bible is the Word of God, and we are commissioned to preach the whole counsel of God and look to the Holy Spirit to fructify that Word – which he gave in the first place through the minds of the writers – then there is scarcely any room for distinction between evangelistic and edifying preaching.

James Packer has been saying that the difference between lecturing and preaching is application. There must always be application of the Word. Yes, there may be a difference in the immediate response to lecturing and preaching (although the Holy Spirit doesn't necessarily desert the lecturer), but the immediate response to the Word may have much, or little, to do with its eventual lodgement in men's hearts. When it takes something like five, ten, fifteen, twenty, twenty-five, thirty, even thirty-five years for some people to come through to Christ under the gentle, or not so gentle, expounding of the Word of God, what are you going to achieve (if I can change the metaphor somewhat) by trying to force its reluctant flower to bloom by high-pressure tactics? Many a man has run away from a situation in which, if he had stayed longer, he would have had a harvest, but that possibility was dissipated by premature departure long before the seed had begun to germinate in stubborn hearts.

Some of you are living on the capital of what others have seen and known. But where is your capital? You will have to show your fruit for any different ways you sponsor from those I am advocating, if they are to be credible. You see here, today, the proliferation of certain simple, comprehensive ideas, emanating from one source. Where in Scotland, today, do you see signs, even vestiges of the fruitful proliferation of other ideas? Within the Establishment – or outside it? I know that there are gimmicks that may be tried, but it was in the second half of 1945 and throughout 1946 that I learned that gimmickry of any sort cannot last, and the only thing that did last, and does, is the solid presentation of the Word of God, washed and watered by costly prayer. 'We will give ourselves to prayer,' said the Apostles, and prayer comes first in that statement in the Acts, and then the Word of God. That's what saved the Church from early extinction; and it was lack of that in my young day which almost caused the extinction of the living Church of Scotland, until God took a hand and gave us back the Word of God and Prayer. What is there to put in their place as sole priority?

One of my most gracious and fruitful contacts in Northern Ireland wrote to me after three years with us and said that the fruits of that ministry will abide with him. It was a great inspiration, he said, to see a Presbyterian Church that 'works' – by which he meant that it was an encouragement to be part of a people who cared for one another in a way that is more generally associated with small gatherings, and to experience fellowship more generally felt in what he calls 'charismatic' churches. (In fact, I would claim that we are more truly charismatic than many churches with the label.) This, he says – referring to us – is a model to work towards, with the most important lesson, the central place of prayer, and the foremost thought in mind, that of 'dying many deaths'. One of the things he would remember with joy, he said, was preaching in our pulpit, and seeing the response of those faces, with the spiritual sensitivity of Drew Tulloch at the organ. All I would say about that is that it has taken forty-one years to produce it – and I didn't start until I was thirty-four. And that, it seems to me, on reflection, may summarize one's expectations of what the ministry of the Word may do when it is copiously watered by the corporate prayers of the people, and is geared towards the establishment of the kind of church which has, in this fitful, changeful world, abiding and perpetuating qualities.

You see, this ministry of over forty-one years has already produced two other ministries of practically thirty years in one place; and there are a few twenty-year ministries and more; then more of fifteen years; and more still of more than ten years.

The fruits of such ministries are vitally and integrally related to its ways. Some, I know, question that, and intend to gain the same results, and fruits, by waiving, or even denying certain of the main principles upon which such ministries have been founded, and would claim that they can achieve the same, and even better, by other ways. Well, we have yet to see them! I am waiting patiently, and humbly, to see them. I, myself, do not believe that there are alternatives to a massive emphasis on the ministry of the Word, and the patterns of prayer-life which (I would say) needs must go along with it. It is easy to pick the flowers one likes, and put them in a vase, and tend them with new, technical means of perpetuating their cut-flower life, but they soon fade, nevertheless, and have to be thrown away, because they do not have roots in soil. Cut flowers in the house, I find, can be a bit of a nuisance, whereas in my tiny conservatory – and more so in the garden – flowers are a longer-lasting delight when they have roots in the soil that one can nourish. You see the point?

Look at the situation today. Look at even the most illustrious congregations, with the most able ministers of moderate persuasion, struggling to maintain a semblance of settled continuity, with practically none of their younger generations having anything vital to do with their congregations beyond primary and junior Sunday Schools, and maybe a short acquaintance with Bible Class and Youth Fellowship; maybe joining the Church, and even becoming elders; but with far more important priorities in their lives than the Kirk. And with each successive generation less and less thirled to the idea of the Church as the centre of their lives, what can the future of such deadening moderateness be? Their ignorance of the Bible is seen in their proneness to espouse any old or new political or social theory that some new-fangled charlatan comes along with; and we find, as is Norman Tebbit's point (and he's no Christian but a shrewd observer), that as soon as the Church is challenged as to its share of blame for the moral decline of the nation, it instantly shies away from the subject to economic considerations, and trots out social theories. The Church adamantly refuses to face the fact, which Karl Marx, with all his theorizing, could never face, that the trouble in the world today is moral and spiritual, not basically social or economic, racial or intellectual. In the face of all this, we have everything to offer. We have the Word watered by prayer, which produces character, and which produces money out of people's own pockets because Christ and his fellowship mean more to them than anything else. We are able to build a community (despite many of its most fruitful members being for ever on their way out to some project of evangelistic or didactic endeavour in some part of the land or the world) which has in it the very solidity which runs counter to all the hair-brained schemes which vainly attempt to gather people together and keep them together for longer than a few weeks or months, or a year or two.

It was my experience of 1946, during no more than nine months of 'Youth for Christ' (started in Gilcomston by Billy Graham in March of that year), which proved to me that that sort of thing, with all its gimmicks, was vastly inferior to the ministry of the Word in church on Sunday. It was then that the systematic Bible expository ministry really began, and the fruit of that ministry was found to be far more related to the solid exposition of the biblical text on Sunday evenings (and mornings, too) than on Saturday nights at our interdenominational youth rallies with all their blazing and blatant attempts to draw people in – including a small army out on the streets with bills persuading them to come in. The growing evidence of that comparison made me wage war, that very same year, with Alan Redpath who was in Aberdeen for three weeks in October. Although a number of people were converted under that campaign – well, we prayed hard for it! – it was clear to me that God had shown me something far superior to an evangelistic pattern of church life, namely, that of a fully evangelical ministry of the Word – I say it again – watered by prayer. When you have seen that – and some of you haven't yet seen it, because you haven't bothered to see it; some of you may be afraid at the cost of it, and I don't wonder at that! – but when you've seen that, you are spoiled for ever for anything else.

I think it has been amply demonstrated for all with eyes to see, that this is the only way forward for our Church in these days, as a living, spiritual body, without which it will fade away and perish. And if what Sinclair Ferguson and Iain Murray of Banner of Truth, and Nigel Cameron of Rutherford House, have sought to do for me and my work this year has any significance at all, it is to bring before the susceptible public the fact that, by the grace of God alone, we have cottoned-on to a good thing. The fact alone that good friends of ours have poured nothing less than a million pounds into the Lord's work in Scotland within fifteen years says something. And it contains all the seeds of a movement of the Spirit which could change not only our Church, but eventually our nation; and spread its benign message far and wide not only throughout the Presbyterian world, but interdenominationally, and until even the political world takes notice. Indeed, if the coming of the Lord himself draws near – and there are many of various persuasions inclined to believe that – then this could eventually have influence on that penultimate act of the grace of God, which must, according to Romans 11, precede the *Parousia*; namely, the conversion of Israel.

Now, you may think I am consumed with megalomania; but if I am, it is, I believe, by the legitimate megalomania wrought in one by the Word of God, and its sole, essential, fructifying agency, the corporate prayers of the people. If you say that I am blinded to all but that, then I am well content, and know that my good Lord, when I meet him face to face, will not hold that against me, or charge me with it, or chastize me for it. So I quote again the famous words, which are all my inspiration: 'And we will give ourselves to prayer, and to the ministry of the Word'.

But now I want to raise a thorny question with no greater intent at this juncture than that of stimulating thought and encouraging what we hope may be inspired speculation on the prospects for the conservative evangelical emphasis, with it systematic biblical expository practice, taking firm hold of the Church of Scotland, and gaining influence, and ultimate authority, to incline the Church to go this fruitful way. It was painfully obvious by our voting numbers at the 1986 General Assembly that we are still a comparatively small minority, although it may have been due to fortuituous circumstances that the sample forward this year was smaller than might indicate our comparative strength throughout the church. Not all conservative evangelical ministers are associated with us, so that I do not know how many conservative evangelicals in toto there may be in the Kirk; But we do remember what a rebuff the plan to demote the *Confession of Faith* was given a year or two ago by a goodly number of presbyteries, doubtless for different reasons, but with sufficient unanimity to afford us considerable encouragement.

A much more serious threat, I think, which seems ever to be looming larger, is the insidious influence of the monstrous regiment of masterful women in their movement to feminize the whole ethos of our worship, and ultimately (one does not doubt) to affect the Scriptures. Although I think we may rejoice at the fruitful service of women, if they keep their due and worthy place, on the other hand if their 'muscle' and the plaudits of the pathetic men enamoured of their intended 'takeover' should lead to an insurgence of them, we may well wonder whether we can continue in a denomination which is ruled by such immoderate souls, who succeed in setting aside the order of nature with regard to the sexes in creation, and in the administration of the Kirk. The question may be: How far and how fast can our cause grow to combat that and other harmful influences? Or, a much deeper question, and to be taken even more seriously: What measure of divine initiative is present among us for this movement I have been talking about to get off the ground nationally? It is surely of God, as the fact alone of several hundred prayer meetings taking place in the Church of Scotland today testifies: forty or fifty years ago there would have been but a handful, if that. This is of God, but is it of God to establish a new ministry in our national Church, or simply to become a faction, formed of a comparatively small number of the total ministers and congregations? Is it the Lord's purpose for us to grow and assume an ever greater measure of influence in the Kirk, or will some moderate or liberal movement yet arise to catch away a majority of semi-evangelical churches in some other ploy, like Iona, enough to keep a liberal church going as a social or political force in the land?

I was reading Conor Cruise O'Brien's saga of Israel and Zionism, entitled *Siege*, and came upon this passage from a letter written from Palestine to his brother in November 1882 by one of the 'Lovers of Israel' movement:

> My final purpose in being here is to take possession, in due course, of Palestine, and to restore to the Jews the political independence, of which they have now been deprived for 2,000 years. Don't laugh! It is not a mirage. The means to achieve this purpose could be the establishment of colonies of farmers of Palestine, the establishment of various kinds of workshops, and industry, and their gradual expansion – in a word, to seek to put all the land, all the industry, in the hands of the Jews. Furthermore, it will be necessary to teach young people, and the future young generations the use of arms.

But that is nothing to my purpose in sharing this quote with you unless you think of 'arms' in terms of spiritual warfare, in which case these last few words are exceedingly significant. But the point of the quote is that it was written, prophetically, more than a hundred years ago, and all that it envisaged for God's chosen people, Israel, has come true in Israel.

The question I ask you, and myself, is: Have we any such hope, or long-term expectation, for the cause of Christ and his Word in our Church and in our land? I believe that nothing less than a conviction of faith that the Lord purposes some major change in our Kirk and in the land is going to sustain us against the odds that are powerfully stacked against us. And it is my desire, practically every day, that the Lord would clarify my vision of the total scene, to see if there is any Word from the Lord which would give us hope that the appalling things our Church is intent upon may one day, within at least the lifetime of the younger men here, be reversed, and the Word of God – let me say it again – watered by corporate prayer assume its full, and true, and fruitful role in our Church and in the nation.

Chapter 7

# Let the Brain Take the Strain (or: The Hail in this Tale Falls Mainly on the Gael)

Ian Mackenzie

*Ian Mackenzie's theological label could be 'SCM', but it is impossible to put labels on this dedicated eccentric whose capacity for lateral and parabolic thinking is well illustrated by his contribution. He went to Edinburgh University to study music and emerged assistant minister at St. Giles where he married the Dean's daughter and preached a farewell sermon on the text 'Ye are not all illegitimate'. Some say he could have had a career as a jazz pianist, but instead he worked for SCM, then for ITV in the religious department at ABC, and was minister at Peterhead before becoming Head of Religious Programmes at BBC Scotland. His swansong from this post was the marathon film series 'The Quest' which both enthralled and infuriated viewers. He now runs an independent production company from his home in Helensburgh.*

The Scots comic actor (a higher class of person than comedian) Robbie Coltrane boasted in *Punch* that he had recently held his own in conversation with the English comic actor Stephen Fry. And, claimed Coltrane, Fry had a brain the size of the Isle of Wight. He had apparently reported this observation to Ned Sherrin, a proponent of *aperçus* more of my generation, who had corrected him: 'The size of England.' On the other hand, the *Guardian* reported the comedian and actor Jimmy Mulville as confining the Fry brain to the size of Kent.

Leaving on one side the cranial magnitude of Mr Fry, we are left with the question: how large, brain-wise, are the Isle of Wight, Kent and England? And, in contrast, Scotland? Which leads, by precisely the sort of jump Scottish, if not English, brains are prone to, to the question: how big a brain has God? For example, is it bigger than Mr Fry's? It cannot, surely, be bigger than the brain of Professor Tom Torrance. This, being in a class of its own, is something we shall return to in due course. The Torrance brain is, of course, a reproductive brain, reproducing other Torrance brains in due season, but so far Godfather Torrance is not intellectually threatened by junior members of the neo-orthodox Mafia littered elegantly around the theological colleges of Scotland. It would be not only out of order, it would be misleading to see anything organized about that. It would, on the other hand, be not only in order but complementary to see deliberate organization behind the means of reproduction, distribution and exchange in relation to another category of brain, glittering gilt at the other end of the theological rainbow. One refers, of course, to the collective brain of the wild goose. To any not familiar with this nomenclature, this is the appellation currently applied to itself by the cybernetic apparatus surmounting *Homo MacLeodus*, in plain English, Iona Man, found on the Herbidean island where George MacLeod's brainchildren proliferate. Since the Torrance brain regarded the MacLeod brain as entirely empty of theology (insult), and the MacLeod brain regarded the Torrance brain as absolutely stuffed with theology (insult), it may be convenient to take these complementary manifestations as spanning the intellectual space occupied by Christian insights in Scotland in the period which affected my generation, and through them influenced the present.

Now, as in a Tolstoy novel, we must fill out the landscape, describe the terrain of major battlefields, and flesh out characters already referred to; after which we shall feel free to introduce other *dramatis personae* who give credibility to a conceptual world by merely existing. What follows is a prologue, an essay and an epilogue.

## Prologue

The Word became Brain. Or do I have this wrong somewhere?
Try again.
In the beginning was the Scottish sermon. Three points.
1. This is not a point. This is a text.
2. That was a text. Don't worry unduly about it. Here is an anecdote. Ho, ho, ho.
3. Lunch awaits us all. God's in His heaven, and all's well that ends well.
Amen.

## The Essay

In which we revert to autobiographical prose. When I was a young student, attending more ecumenical student Christian conferences in Swanwick than would be thought healthy for a young Presbyterian, an Anglican divine in a swishing brown dressing-gown said:

'Ah, you're *Scottische*. I do so admire the *intellectual rigour* of your theology and your preaching. We Anglicans inhabit, alas, a rather – ah – emotional ambience.'

My jaw, so far as I can recall, dropped. It has remained in the unretracted position ever since.

I am simply at a loss to know how there arose the myth of the austere Scottish theological intellect. Where *is* this thing? Let us examine the possible locations: the universities; the Iona Community; the manses; the pulpits (this might seem to overlap with the manses, but that would be to ignore the transformation from the quiet intellectual tadpole of the Saturday night's manse study to the jumping rhetorical frog of the Sunday morning's children's address); the ecumenical movement; and the homes of the people. Finally, inasmuch as he is an honorary Scot, we might seek out this austere intellect in God.

In order.

The universities. It is alleged that, from a time shortly after Plato, being a member of the academic staff involved a commitment to truth. Indeed, that long golden age extended to my first year at Edinburgh, when membership of the general arts course involved sitting with hundreds of other ex-schoolkids at the feet of Profs Pares (History), Macmurray (Philosophy) and Gray (Economics, Poetry and Jokes), each of whom in the course of a lecture described an arc of such rhetorical synchronicity as would adorn Further Education in the Elysian Fields.

These were, of course, pre-Thatcher, and their like is, as decisively as the dinosaurs, extinct. Their successors, or a significant number of their successors, are the academic yuppies who are obliged to make productivity their god. Publish or be damned. Improve your student/hour ratio, your exam-graph curve, your essay-marking velocity – above all, your publication quota. At the next department meeting, confess your failure to deliver a department-supporting cost-cutting scheme as part of a new strategy for the university's economic survival; then fall on your sword and die. And by die, we don't mean death and resurrection; we mean die, goodbye and good night.

But *theology*, surely, is different. That really *is* about truth. Indeed (*sotto voce*), is it not about resurrection? 'Ay, there's the rub.' To die, to ratiocination, perchance to rise to poetry. This dilemma was not resolved in my theological training. My theological training introduced me to Scottish intellectual austerity via the following ingredients. Professor Micky Porteous was in love. He wooed with chivalrous finesse two amours: on the one hand, the Old Testament; on the other, the New College, on to whose faculty he was craftily manipulating some of the best brains in the theological trade. And he was no mean manipulator, as he demonstrated in his Old Testament lectures. Lectures? They fell (apart) into two parts: anecdotes about the Confessing Church in Nazi Germany; and dramatic reconstructions of Old Testament battles. When I say dramatic, I mean melodramatic: ham acting at its finest. Peter Snow of 'Newsnight', eat your heart out, as you see Micky (né Norman) Porteous, not the largest of men, hurl himself from one corner of the room where he has just graphically been a Philistine army, to the contrary corner, where he proceeds to be a lonely prophet on a rock.

Then I adduce those who were hired to make us think objectively about the New Testament. Some hope. On my left, the silver-tongued J. S. (Jamie) Stewart. No less a one than R. D. Kernohan, the retired editor of *Life and Work*, wrote recently in the *Glasgow Herald* that J. S. Stewart was the only twentieth-century preacher to make an impact beyond the 'diminished minority in the pews'. *Preacher*, note. Yet here was this pulpit bugler leading us into the analytical entrails of the texts. Oh no, he wasn't. There he was, gazing out the windows at the angels invisible to us, but not to him, as they clawed to gain admittance and grab an earful of silver-toned action. That market, however, was cornered already in notebooks by assembled stenographers, wives to a man of American Southern Baptist theological students, one of whom, in my presence at a college lunch, leaned over a gangrenous Scotch trifle to ask Professor Stewart, 'Sir, who would you say was the *second* greatest preacher in Scotland?' The great man blushed, but, I regret to report, failed to push his pudding into the inquiring mouth.

Now on my New Testament right, enter Robin Barbour. His thing wasn't preaching, if by preaching you mean the adjectival equivalent of Liberace. The Barbour contribution was angst. He was a lovely man (well, so was Jamie, so were they all). He enfolded us in that wonderfully boyish grin, as, with preternatural anguish, he hoisted us with the diverse petards of St. Paul. Barbour on Paul on freedom was barboured wire, indeed. But I rather liked that. It related to real life. It also related to Paul, one of the less uncomplicated brains one has encountered. But: austere? Detached? Clinical? Objective? Robin Barbour, one of the most modest and accessible saints and mystics of the century, is as capable of detachment as a hedgehog trapped at the top of a hundred-foot-high Scots Pine!

You will perceive that I loved these men. You couldn't not; they were so obviously in love themselves. Porteous loved the Old Testament. Stewart and Barbour were head over heels in love with the New. What about the practical application of all that in the real world whose windmills we were about to confront? The Professor or Practical Theology was William Tindall. Practical he was not. Theological, he was not. A wonderful man he was. I think he was the purest Professor of Practical Theology that Scotland has ever had, because he had no respect whatever for the subject. He didn't believe it existed. Certainly he never lectured about it. What he was was human; and in those emotionally strenuous years his war experiences and his advice on which side of the cup to drink out of in a house of suspect hygiene enabled me, at least to remain human. He made me smile. He made me laugh. He was anecdotally relentless. Could one ask for more? I understood why he had become, in the Second World War, Field Marshall Montgomery's personal chaplain. Probably it was his keeping Monty relaxed that beat Rommel, and, by extension, Hitler, in the end.

Now, however, we come to the heart of the matter. Theology itself. The fulcrum. The Holy Grail. The inner sanctum of pure thought. All that.

It's a contest. Always was. Always will be. On my left, Socrates; on my right Mick Jagger, crossed with Albert Einstein.

Socrates was in my time cast twice. First John Baillie. He was a thinker whose lucidity had the sparkle of a Highland burn. Come to think of it, my whole thesis is liable to collapse if I dwell on him, for he had a logical brain, and didn't apologize for using it. I heard him preach once at a university service. He didn't ever want theological *agreement*, he said. In heaven, he would be as helpless without theological disagreement as Yehudi Menuhin would be without his violin. But, in the last resort, he falls, austere-brainwise, because he was haunted by the poetry of lost things. His published prayers have the ache of poetic economy; and in his last sermon at a New College communion, he apologized to us students. 'I have failed,' he said, lantern-jawed, 'my life has lacked joy.'

He was succeeded in the Socratic role by the other John: Macintyre. He carried that role too far, by a whisker. His long silent gazes out the window were not to perceive angels, but to convince us he was in deadly earnest about *not* telling us what to think. He was creating a space so embarrassing that one of us would *have* to jump in. Which we did. Embarrassingly. Whereupon John Macintyre would utter a funny. And his funnies were funny. Both these Johns were frauds. They pretended to be ruthless strippers of irrationality. But it was only a striptease. Always, underneath, were the everlasting arms. They were in love with God.

Not, however, as vocally as Thomas F. Torrance. His brain was indecently large. And, if you ignored its blind spots (proportion, objectivity, openness), spectacularly efficient. He was the biggest fraud of all – but only because he was the biggest everything of all. He was just the biggest. His fraud was thus: he talked *as if* theology was scientific. For this, the word 'phooey' is inadequate. The fact of the matter was that Torrance was loopily and enchantingly bowled over by a vision of Christ. His heart said, 'Wowee.' But because he *wasn't* (unlike Mick Jagger or Pavarotti) a singer with a big larynx, but was, like Albert Einstein, a poet with a big brain, he wrote an epic love poem to the universe, c/o J. C., Esq., and carved it up into lectures on Christology. Look at that word. Let it sink in. Did Jesus get born, walk, talk, die, for the invention of a word like Christology? Fortunately, as I've said, what came out was not a system of scientific logic. I was one of the beneficiaries. I can never think of Christ in a dull way again. Like J. S. Stewart, Tom Torrance was a preacher, not a teacher. Or, and here we come to the point, a preacher and *therefore* a teacher; for if Christ *is* risen, then how do you teach about *that* other than by rising? By being in love, and making it contagious?

The answer is, there is no other way. You can't begin to understand a soufflé unless you see it, just out of the oven, risen. And you can't fully savour what makes it different from a bread and butter pudding unless you actually taste it. Textual skills in themselves teach you about two things: texts and textual skills. That these are desirable is not denied. 'Facts are chiels that winna ding', and the more facts known the better. The argument isn't about that. The argument is whether it is the job of a university faculty, even of theology, to teach anything else, like, say, resurrection? Widely as I am roaming, I balk at going over *that* old debate about whether preachers should be reared in university faculties or church colleges. I would only remark that New College, at the stage in its evolution at which I experienced it, had a perplexing ambiguity, partaking of elements both academic and ecclesiological, and that, I believe, is what made it fascinating. Even as I loitered within that ambiguity, intrigued by its contradictions, stimulated by the resultant tensions and lunacies, I saw the tide turn. Alec Cheyne, church historian, pellucid to a degree, would help you to a degree; and James Barr, who joined Norman Porteous, dissected Old Testament texts like the Fraserburgh girls of my childhood gutting herring. Fast and clean. No sermons there, either. But, the *cognoscenti* protest, it is not the job of a university faculty to teach preaching. Precisely. Or, on the other hand, why not?

If this were a Tolstoy, or any, novel, one would outline in equivalent detail the Iona *dramatis personae* before following through into manses, pulpits and the homes of the people the effects of both traditions. In this little *pensée*, I have devoted disproportionately more space to the New College scene because the Iona scene is better known. I knew Iona best at the time I knew New College. On the basis of two summers and an Easter organizing the Community music, one had ample opportunity to listen, look and participate, and my conclusion was and remains that the neatly diagrammatic antithesis cherished by each institution about the other was mythical. I found the New College ambience as emotionally conditioned as a Susan Howatch novel and I found the Iona discourse as intellectually strenuous as a faculty debate. George MacLeod's

brain was, although different, every bit as prodigious as Tom Torrance's. The encephalon of his deputy, Ralph Morton, was at least
as sharp as John Macintyre's. As with New College, the practical
theology aspect was conspicuous by its absence: building an abbey
had little to do with ordinary people's lives. But the Community
had four colossal plus factors, in terms of education: first, the logic-
breaking numinosity of the environment; secondly, the worship;
thirdly, the communal living and round table dialogue; and fourthly
the preaching. Two or three generations of future preachers experienced existentially what can be done with words in a worship context. But then, one hundred and fifty miles to the east, Tom Torrance
and some of his colleagues were demonstrating, in a lecture context,
something remarkably similar. (I beg to differ from the Kernohan
estimate of J. S. Stewart, whose sermons, though luminous, lacked
a creative tension between logic and emotion.) Now, then, how did
all this inspiration follow through?

By and large, it didn't. Why? Because both Torrance and MacLeod
covered their tracks, or had them covered by their respective institutions. It didn't suit the strategy of a church college, desperate to
be accepted as a university faculty, to advertise the fact that its
principal luminary, who was attracting every year scores of fee-
paying foreign students, and, to boot, publishing like mad, was a
wild authoritarian Romantic preacher of the poetic school whose
lectures, brilliant and haunting, bore as much relation to academic
detachment as a forest fire to conservation. Nor did it suit the
strategy of the Iona Community to advertise the fact that its principal
luminary – and also, on relentless American lecture tours, main
money-making agent – was a wild authoritarian Celtic mystic whose
maverick instinctual forays into the alchemy of the cosmic cauldron
bore as much relation to most of the Community's horizontal socialist instincts as Lord Longford's concern for prisoners to the rank
and file of the Police Federation.

Therefore both geniuses were not only undersold, but hidden
under the counter. Tom, the wild preacher, whose heart and voice
sang with a love for a wild Christ, was converted, or converted
himself, into the iron theologian of the right, and the Kirk's ecclesiastical strategist and theological mugger, for example beating down
by Moderatorial *viva voce* a poor elder whose crime was a desire to
meet God in a second baptism in the Pentland Firth. And George
was converted, or converted himself, into the iron apostle of the
left, the Community strategist, hewing, with inadequate research,
pamphlets on political issues about which the Community's members might be expected to form a consensus. The result was a waste.
For most ministers eschewed both strategies. But, because the one
thing both men, and both traditions, offered directly, namely seismic
preaching and praying, had been, as it were, apologized for, most

ministers felt it inappropriate to attempt to make the earth move. Now it may well be that many would have failed in the attempt. But not to try? Why, then, be ordained to preach at all? Because, comes the correct reply, the preacher's job is not to impose private religious perspectives via rhetoric on defenceless congregations. To do this is to fall prey to one of the many versions of the pulpit personality cult. The preacher's job (this sanitized view holds) is facing, with the congregation, the open Bible, to share with them what is revealed in the tradition contained there, and to receive humbly the word of truth, judgement, forgiveness, broken sacramentally in the context of the whole liturgy. And the preacher's contribution to that process is to use the textual skills in which he or she has been trained, as teacher, not guru. Now that may *sound* all right (actually, it doesn't, it sounds pretty boring) but that is simply not what happens. Apart from a handful of clergy who are probably, after their first parish, going to return to academic life, most preachers drop their linguistic and textual interests – and most of their doctrinal interests – if not after their last exam, then after their first hard winter under the pressures of parish life. They have recourse then to the sermon as a vital person-to-person communication at the centre of the whole pastoral situation. But by now, too late in the day, they find that their theological training did not train them how to preach.

The result? In the manses, lack of innate conviction that preaching is a justified activity in a virile twentieth-century managerial ministry. In the pulpits, lack of a language flexibly comprehensive enough to meet the scale of the congregation's emotional and intellectual need. In other words, lack of a serviceable rhetoric, that is a rhetoric with sufficient poetic variables. Preaching *is* poetry, or it is nothing. And, let it be noted, poetry need not be – indeed the best poetry isn't – 'poetic', any more than music need be 'tunes'. Bach and Shostakovich didn't write 'tunes'. Sinewy counterpoint attains an unself-conscious foundation-shaking resonance by pursuing the truth. Unfortunately, what all too often fills the interstices of unprepared sermons is chat. There are exceptions. In the church I attend, both the previous and the present minister combine rational exposition with metaphor. And I could list, straight off, a couple of dozen pulpits which offer this essential amalgam. But then, my list falls off the various edges of wall-to-wall cliché, topical conversation, fundamentalist parrot language, or emotional hype. Which leaves us with the ecumenical movement; the homes of the people; and God.

The ecumenical movement has been largely a linguistic wasteland. I don't mean that in its conferences and services it has not sometimes evoked wonderful sermons and speeches. But that is in private. What it produces for public consumption is agenda-drone, draft-prose, sub-committee synthesis, plenary syntax, translatese jargon. It is now too middle-aged to have kept, and not yet old enough to have recovered, its original thrust, its willingness to be riskily inspiring rather than conscientiously correct. There, for the moment, we will leave the home of global fudge-speak, and enter the homes of the people. Ah. At last. This is where there is real language and real theology. Why? Because this is where God is. Here he is to be found, nakedly trailing his clouds of incarnational glory, uncensored by institutional strategies. Where the brain of the university theologian can be inhibited by the need to prove itself academically; where the brains of pioneering outfits like Iona can be inhibited by the need to prove themselves sociologically; where the brain of the poor hard-pressed minister, tied umbilically to Kirk fabric and finance can be inhibited by the need to prove itself managerially; the human brain to which all these efforts are supposed to be directed is, in the private (and communal) space of its home, office, factory, army barracks, prison cell, kitchen sink, long-distance lorry cabin, aircraft flight-deck or hospital ward, confronted by the age-old reality: God, self and A. N. Other. That is where prayer is. That is where revelation is. That is where Christ repeatedly dies and rises: in the brain of the average Scot. And that is why the average minister or priest need not despair.

But God's brain: how big? It is *that* big. *That* small. *That* unique. The size of Robbie Coltrane's, Stephen Fry's, Tom Torrance's, George MacLeod's, yours and mine.

It may be considered that talking about God having a brain is a little anthropomorphic. I would put it differently. It is entirely anthropomorphic. There is no other way we can be. That is why we have preachers, and that is presumably why Jesus, as someone convincingly man-like, is given a place of some centrality in the Bible, the tradition and our preaching.

When people shrink from images which attribute characteristics to God, what they may be shrinking from is the thought that there is a God at all. The idea of the existence of God is a very disturbing one, and as much fundamentalist as agnostic aggression proceeds from a fear of shouldering the full burden of that idea. To face a living God is indeed a formidable undertaking; and to live with the consequences of such a Being (of whatever form) being able to out-think us must be terrifying to brains which rest on the security of human logic. Over a decade and a half I have had the privilege of observing in close focus two brains. They developed in conditions not unlike a controlled experiment, and in the context I described above as offering the most direct access to the activity of God: the homes of the people. In this case, I am the people, and the home is that of my wife and myself. The two brains are those of a daughter who is dyslexic and a son who is not. The observation has not, of course, been casual: it cannot be with parents. The factor of deep love enables one to some extent to have access to the inside of these brains, in a way imperfectly but not foolishly analogous to the way that the love bond between God and us enables us to cross boundless transdimensional vastness and have communion with God. To balance this emotional factor, my wife, by profession a trained Froebel teacher, has over many years trained to become a teacher specializing in dyslexia, thus affording me conceptual and technical insights comparable to those offered by theology in the study of God. Finally, as background, it has been fortuitous that both children have above average intelligence and direct comparisons can therefore be made.

In summarizing the difference between the operations of these two brains one is bound to over-simplify, but certain conclusions are not in doubt. The dyslexic brain works largely laterally, the other one in a linear pattern. This is not to deny to the dyslexic considerable powers of analysis and fluent speech – she is a particularly accurate raconteuse – nor to the non-dyslexic a strong imagination – jazz and writing science fiction are his principal voluntary activities – so we are not looking at stereotyped caricatures (I leave on one side the gender distinction). Nevertheless, the distinction is clear: one brain works more by intuition, emotion, visualization, the other works more by logical sequencing and verbalization. In other words, the well-known distinction between brains biased towards the logical (usually left) side and those biased towards the intuitive (usually right) side. Dr Harry Chasty is the Studies Director of the Dyslexia Institute. He is no arid theoretician or romantic crusader. He was the highly successful headmaster of one of Ireland's best-known public schools, and a psychologist, before giving his life to this work. I interviewed him for the BBC film series 'The Quest' and, in response to an admittedly leading question, he conjectured it as perfectly possible that Jesus, an obvious visualizer, might, like Albert Einstein, have been dyslexic, while Paul, an equally obvious verbalizer, was clearly not. Dr Chasty was not biased towards either. He said, 'The church needed a Paul to systematize the insights of Jesus for the verbalizers.' The problem in the modern world is this, however: the entire educational system is geared to the verbalizer. It is this, not some handicap of intelligence, that can disenfranchise the one in fifteen or twenty of the population who is dyslexic. Apply this to our theological faculties and pulpits, and ask the obvious question.

Leaving specific learning difficulties on one side, it is open to commonplace observation that two parallel sets of tradition of expression present themselves: the lyrical and the forensic. The romantic and the classical. The rhetorical and the analytical. The intuitive and the inductive. The speculative and the factual. The poetic and the prosaic. The mythical and the realistic. The subjective and the objective, the parabolic and the argumentative. And only a reader with acute literary myopia would have failed to note that this essay has divided stylistically into two sections; in the first, I 'let myself go' emotionally, adjectivally, subjectively. In this second part, I am attempting a factual description and analysis. I may not be skilful in either style; but I feel at home in both, and I have used both parts of my brain in most of the jobs and situations I have encountered.

Most of us are able to do this, so most of us attain a reasonable balance in work and life. A balanced approach is likely if we can synthesize the two halves of our brain. It goes without saying, therefore, that if God can by hypothesized as having that which is best, from our perspective, described as a brain, it must be supremely whole and balanced in terms of emotion and intellect. And yet. The utterly intriguing question at the heart (a word I have eschewed till this point) of the gospel is this. If the Word was sufficient, both self-sufficient and sufficiently able to deal with us *qua* Word, why become flesh? If a fastidious Logos could cope, why throw itself off the safe edge of infinite rationality into the irrational quagmire of instinct-governed flesh?

If preaching is not about that, is it, whatever else it is, Christian preaching? If teaching is not about that, is it, whatever else it is, teaching connecting directly with Christian preaching? The great thing about a Torrance or a MacLeod is that they were not fastidious. They were constantly throwing themselves off the edge of their own logic in pursuit of these questions. And the most existentially perilous preacher I heard in my lifetime, Harry Whitley of St. Giles, as a result of his Catholic Apostolic upbringing, knew of no way to preach other than on the basis that Christ might actually turn up at *this* service in ultimate judgement. Each of these men preached and prayed, as if the partition between our dimension and the dimension where God ultimately operates is tissue thin, and each associated that threatening and thrilling thinness with the figure of Christ. For each of them the word 'Christ' had a cosmic ring and the implication, explicated in paradox after paradox, was that at the heart of the Christian assessment of where the human race now stands is some stupendous transaction which crosses the limits of our normal logic. These are difficult matters for ordinary language and therefore it is entirely understandable that brains of a linear set not given to intuitive utterance, let alone poetry, have difficulty in tackling them. But I find preaching which does not make the attempt not very interesting, because it is not doing the one thing which is its *raison d'être*, namely, still, to do what John Milton attempted: justify the ways of God to men.

I return to the question: if, God, as Logos, was self-sufficient, why the adventure into 'flesh', of which the act of the original

Creation can be seen as the precursor? Because a true balance is not static but dynamic. A spinning top which stops rotating loses its balance. If a continuation of the crude metaphor may be allowed, the balance between the two sides of God's brain is not balance if it atrophies in self-satisfaction. The best analogy I know is that of art. The creative artist is constantly stretching the categories, pushing out the conceptual and technical boat. Art is that which gives form to dangerous expeditions into the formless. The artist lets his or her lateral side go, lets emotion take risks, steps off ledge after ledge, but the linear part of the brain is in hot pursuit to redeem through discipline, intelligence, intellectual effort.

My suggestion is that God cannot continue to be God, cannot, perhaps, fully become God, without his creation – from our point of view, us – leading him into vulnerability. And preaching is one vulnerable but committed expression of God the artist: the New Testament expression, the expression on the paradoxical face of Christ; that expression which can show both God and us what vulnerability means.

So which has the bigger brain, the Church in Scotland, or in England? The people on Iona or in the universities? Professors or ministers? Laymen or laywomen?

The wrong question. Brain quality is not about size. I have known cats and dogs whose brains, developed in loving and stimulating family environments, became tuned to a high degree of social harmony, with intuition and certain trained functions brought to a responsive vulnerable balance. Humans are capable of more, but a dynamic, harmonious dissonance-resolving counterpoint is still the way. We are capable of constant transforming – a better word, possibly, than 'reforming' with its historical overtones of politico-legal ecclesiastical conflict.

It was, of course, nonsense for my Swanwick interlocutor with the swishing habit to describe English churchmanship as emotional and Scottish as intellectual. At their best, Anglicans achieve a cohesive artistic amalgam of liturgical treasure in word and music stretched by honest prophetic utterance in preaching – some of the most intellectually trenchant sermons I've heard, in both exegetical and eschatological terms, have come from Anglican cathedral pulpits – sermons of which my Free Kirk ancestors would have been proud.

And the Scottish tradition of both preaching and theological teaching was, at its best, an artistic synthesis of form and content, of emotion and logic, which went about as far as the human brain can do, at this stage in its evolution, to explore that cosmos of inner and outer space which is reality seen by us, still, as puzzling reflections in a mirror. I have for long realized my unpayable debt to my ex-curricular teachers: the preachers Adam Burnett, George MacLeod, Harry Whitley and my own father.

But I look back now, with nostalgia and great respect, at those men of my New College student days who were so absurdly in love with their subject, their college, their God and, I suppose, with us. I feel sorry for their successors, children of a lesser God: of efficiency. And I pray that the Iona brain, originally a Celtic-led nuclear explosion of the MacLeod sun, will not evaporate in the day of the goose, into sentimentality on the one hand or practical mundanity on the other. There are hopeful signs that the Community has returned to its Celtic interests; of which the very use of the 'Wild Goose' label is one. But watch it: keep that goose wild.

There remains, of course, the question of whether God, and therefore a brain of God, exists in the first place. My brain is not athletic enough to leap across that logical chasm. Nor is anyone else's that I have evidence of; not even scientists from Albert Einstein to Stephen Hawking.

On the other hand, if Stephen Fry were to get round to it . . .

## Epilogue

Another comic actor got round to it. As a Cambridge undergraduate the Scottish politician Ian Lang trod the boards and was, it is claimed, funny. There is, however, no evidence that he was attempting to be funny when, in September 1991, he spoke in Bavaria. As Secretary of State for Scotland, Ian Lang made a speech in which his hosts hoped he would align Scottish independence aspirations with theirs. And pigs fly. The *Glasgow Herald* gave prominence to the fact that Mr Lang quoted the Bible to his Bavarian audience. 'In my Father's house are many mansions' was his reference; and he proceeded to use this text as a prop for the concept of Europe as having unity through diversity. Therefore, he argued, the UK, unlike Federal Germany, needed to retain its integrated status. Therefore, unlike Bavaria, Scotland needed not to have serious devolution or independent representation in Europe.

Her Majesty's Secretary, *representing* a country which has centuries of traditional respect for scripture, for the ceremonials of death and for the hope of a life thereafter with God, to quote for a banal political purpose the text used most commonly to ease the aching heart at the moment of maximum pain, reveals a lack of intuition so remarkable as to constitute some kind of record.

Lest his audience had missed the point, Her Majesty's biblical student from St. Andrew's House lurched into a further lifting of the veil: 'If heaven can accommodate diversity, then surely so can we in the European Community.'

But not we of the United Kingdom? We need detain ourselves no longer with that particular speech, which may, after all, have been drafted by a civil servant who, being a devout elder of some church, had caught the habit of mixing politics and religion from the contagious pulpit diffusions of his minister.

The reason I allowed myself to be detained thus long by a fatuity is that its inherent confusion reflects a fundamental confusion in religious institutions about the locus of institutional identity, and this confusion has its roots in an uncertainty about the identity of God. Is God cosmic soup, and is our best hope that we will become part of a benign cosmic soup?

The whole point can't be argued here in a postscript to an essay. But the bitterest ecclesiastical imbroglios of my lifetime in Scotland were brewed in the cauldron of this confusion. The ecumenical movement espoused the goal of what it called an 'organic' unity. This in contrast to a federal model. If people didn't come to blows about it, that was only because nastier weapons were at hand. The Bishops' Report and the Tirrell affair were only two of the more headlined episodes in the murky story of a couple of decades of all-out Scottish Christian warfare in the 1950s and 1960s, in which Christians fought Christians. Over what? Over a *structural model*. One of many ironies was that those who most piously used the rhetoric of spirituality in support of organic unity, citing not only the Holy Spirit as being on their side, but Christ himself, on the basis of his supposed Johannine prayer, and pronounced maledictions on the federalists as being anti-Christ, were actually those most governed not by a spiritual, but a political image, that of a specific administrative form of machinery. I saw it all from the sidelines, but I saw it from very *close* sidelines, both in Scotland and in England: and if I once sighed deeply while being prayed at with the phrase, 'Father, may they all be as one as we are one', I sighed a thousand times. Because: what does 'one' *mean*?

John Donne put it beautifully, but he put it, I think, wrongly Every man *is* an island. We come, we go, alone. But the sea does not only separate islands, it joins them. The human race, and especially the Celtic race, is a sea-going, flying, travelling race, and the human brain, especially the Celtic brain, is designed to operate largely through intuition, which is why the grip of Roman and Calvinist logic on Scottish and especially Highland and Island spirituality has been such a disaster. The human brain in the human body – certainly in Scotland – is designed to move strongly, determinedly, individualistically; but through a troubled yet educated history it has learned to co-operate in ever widening circles without losing its roots. The sea of life forming, fracturing, re-forming beneath us, joins our brains in a communicative loop which feeds back and transforms brains into spirits. The sea of death that appears to separate us may be but another channel of communication, like the invisible waves of sound or the unheard waves which appear to form matter itself. The eternal spirit which the Bible has in the beginning brooding over the impossible possibility of chaos, must have brain power complex enough to dwarf and enclose an infinite variety of networks, but as it seeks relationship with our vulnerable, fragile individuality, I cannot believe the ultimate result is to reduce all to a cosmic soup, a flat calm ocean, an even unity, a sludge, or even a haggis. In the end, I trust the brain of God to keep us all in the evolving communication of truth till we see things not as puzzling reflections in a mirror, but face to face. Ah! For, yes, look around you. The hidden brain is miracle enough. But whence, pray, comes that vulnerable face you love? And which face exactly reproduces another?

*Chapter 8*

# Authority Structures in the Church

## Michael Hare Duke

*Michael Hare Duke sounds like every Presbyterian's idea of a bishop, but thinks more deeply and creatively than any stereotype. He has been active in clinical theology, when he was a vicar in Nottingham, and prominent in mental health organizations in Scotland. Within his own Scottish Episcopal Church he has been responsible for starting the 'non-stipendiary' ministry and furthering the cause of women's ordination, and is now its senior bishop. His interest in peace led him to believe that the best way to engage in discussion on nuclear weapons was to learn the jargon of strategic studies. In addition he travelled widely in the former Eastern bloc. Lest this makes him sound an entirely serious person, it should be pointed out that he has invented an ecumenical board game on the lines of Monopoly. In the following chapter on authority structures he reveals his capacity to question traditional models and adapt them for contemporary use.*

## Authority, Morale and Mission

I am aware of a malaise in the Church at the moment. Among the clergy morale is low; lay people ask whether the Church has lost its way. The last decade has seen some damaging dents in its image, particularly in the Anglican communion. There were, for instance, the uncertainties surrounding Terry Waite, the Archbishop of Canterbury's special envoy. A romantic figure who had achieved some remarkable bits of negotiation, he scored high in the personality stakes at the end of 1986. Then there was the shock of his disappearance and after that a steady process of detraction. Had he been a tool of the Americans, caught up into the Irangate scandal? Had he ignored advice and put himself imprudently at risk? Investigative journalism has ferreted out and reported with something of a sneer, a story of Lambeth spending £12,000 on negotiations for his release.

In England the long-drawn-out game of 'bait the bishops' took a tragic downward turn in the whole affair of the Crockford preface. This is one symptom of a society where every kind of leadership is thought fair game for attack. The most obvious example is the ritual of Prime Minister's question time in the House of Commons. This has damaging lessons. It makes leaders defensive, eager to use their power to conceal anything which might be a weapon for opponents. Yet in politics, after all the emotion, there is the possibility of blood-letting at a general election. In the Church, clergy, bishops and archbishops are in post for life or until they chose to move. This makes the confrontational model unproductive and harmful to the health of the whole institution. We have adopted the habit of lashing out in personal terms but do not know how to get back from extreme expressions of hostility. Hence perhaps the suicide of the author of the Crockford preface who found himself further out than he had ever intended and with no means of withdrawal.

There was a time when authority went with office. An archbishop would never be attacked by an official publication of his own church. The structures held, and if there were disagreements courtesy, if not charity, was maintained.

Since the eighteenth century we have been developing a society in which individuals have been taught to value their own opinions and to be cowed by nobody. Within the Church this gains theological respectability from a doctrine of the Holy Spirit. If his voice is to be heard in the company of all the baptized, perhaps even within the whole of humanity, we cannot attribute a special quality to the utterances of a clerical hierarchy. We have institutionalized this view by a revolution in church government throughout the Anglican communion where synods have developed composed of three houses, bishops, clergy and laity, each with equal powers of initiation or veto.

Along with the personal authority of office, we have lost the confidence in the traditional use of both the Bible and the teachings of the Church. We have not yet found how to replace them.

It takes time to rediscover the Bible as a rich and encouraging resource when handled in new ways. If we read the text of the Bible, particularly in the familiar language of the authorized version, and then assume that the literal meaning which we hear is what the passage is telling us to do, then the Bible can be misleading. It will make us less able to understand God's call and may well become a barrier to those who are seeking for faith in their own generation. If, however, we take the trouble to understand what the writers were originally saying in their own context and translate it into our situation, then there is much which speaks powerfully and hopefully of God's way with his world.

Similarly, our understanding of traditional church teaching needs to be transformed. This may prove contentious because there is often a high emotional investment on all sides when change is discussed. A relatively minor issue may serve as a case study.

Some years ago, during the papal visit to Ireland, there was a report of the Pope aboard his plane flying, to celebrate mass at the great healing centre at Knock. 'At the moment,' said the commentator, 'he's having breakfast.' Listening to this, a group of Anglicans and Roman Catholics reflected on the enormous shift implied in that statement. They had all been brought up with the conviction that no food or drink must pass the lips of the devout communicant after midnight on the day in which he was to receive communion, let alone be the celebrant at a mass. What had once seemed a vital principle had gone and the Pope was having breakfast.

There still exist in the Episcopal Church the 'Bishops' rules on fasting' which date from that earlier period. Recently I was fascinated to find them quoted in the newsletter of a particular congregation. From internal evidence, I guessed that the lay editor was using them to rebuke the priest who had proposed a congregational coffee session before a late Sunday morning eucharist. Apart from surprise at the fact that the document was quoted, everything seemed out of gear. In the days when those regulations were framed, nobody would have dreamt of criticizing a rector. Furthermore, the bishop's regulations were written in a time when smoking was regarded as a pleasant indulgence which might be given up for Lent. The climate of opinion has changed utterly and there are few who would now regard smoking as a harmless activity.

A trivial example perhaps, but it illustrates the cross-currents at work in our thinking. Yet this leaves us in a quandary. If there are no infallible gurus who have a certain and unchallengeable line to the mind of God, and at the same time the old formulae have lost their guarantee and must be reinterpreted in the light of contemporary understanding, are we then without any authority? Is it appropriate for any individual to challenge their rector or denounce their bishop? Certainly that is what some people fear is being said, yet they then find themselves in the paradoxical situation of defending the threatened system of authority by attacking the rector or bishop who refuses to fulfil the old role of supporting a guaranteed revealed belief system.

The problems of authority and changing tradition appear writ large in the struggle about the ordination of women. Here they have implications for action. Do those who believe that ordination is right demand movement, satisfying their own conscience; or do they hold back and, because of the fear of splitting the Church, become party to another kind of injustice? This is a problem which will be much in the fore in the discussions of the Lambeth fathers.

It would be false to suggest that there is a stark choice between authority and chaos. The dilemma has been with Christianity since the beginning. The first believers saw in Jesus the challenge to a closed system of religious practice which demanded obedience to laws about diet, the keeping of the Sabbath, the purity of the race. This had been the way in which the Jewish people had preserved their identity. Christians proclaimed that the Word had become flesh, replacing the prescriptive demands of the Law. Furthermore, his spirit was given to believers to help them understand his will in their own lives. Following that line St. Francis declared: 'I have done what was mine to do: may Christ teach you what you are to do.'

Such freedom can be very demanding and sometimes it may seem safer to return to a hierarchical leadership. How do you manage a church where everybody claims to be led by the spirit, yet has different perceptions? In the struggle to resolve this problem the clergy and laity have a number of conflicting expectations and these in part underlie the serious malaise in the Church. There has been so much emphasis upon the role of the laity that the full-time clergy wonder what is left for them to do. Sometimes the laity, in exercising their new-found freedom, have reversed roles and speak at church gatherings in the tones of papal infallibility. Others on both sides have resented the changing situation and diagnosed it as faithlessness.

The theological language may obscure the fact that this is not an experience unique to the Church. It is part of the contemporary scene where there is confusion about leadership in a time of change. As ordinary citizens faced with an economic problem or political instability, we are tempted to opt for strong leadership which will take responsibility and solve the problem for us. Because, however, the problem is infinitely complicated, no leader who assumes power on those terms can actually deliver what is promised. The disappointed followers are quickly out for blood. The leader then attempts to defend his or her position by an increasingly authoritarian stance which can degenerate into a battle of personalities. Instead of turning our attention to the fact that there is an enormous problem which requires everyone's collaboration to tackle, we are invited to take sides in a gladiatorial combat.

We see one aspect of this problem in our own country where the politics of certainty are dividing the nation. In America there is the difficulty of finding credible presidential candidates under a system which every four years imagines that the nation will find a new Moses to lead them to the promised land. Impossible expectations are focused on a leader, yet no candidate has a chance of election if he or she exposes the impossibility of the demand.

After the Jews returned from exile they struggled to understand how power could be exercised and from their experience emerged the idea of 'the humble', the unpretentious leaders, people who knew that they were poor. They are the total opposite of the 'mighty' in today's world, the thrusting executive or the ruthless party bureaucrat – the two types from East and West who are mirror-images of one another. The biblical insight suggests that they have mistaken the use of power. Instead, it offers the vision of a God who exalts the humble and meek. This humility is born of self-mistrust, not overweaning confidence. Yet it does not lead to paralysis in action because it is based upon a faith in God. This allows the humble to acknowledge the goodness in others and to work with them; they are not in the business of competition. In this way, it is possible to maximize the qualities of the whole group.

By contrast we have developed a system in which mistrust is a characteristic of our social, political, financial and religious dealings. Every treaty is scrutinized on the assumption that it contains a trick to pull a fast one. With cynical realism, we remind ourselves that there are 'no free lunches', the wise are those who are quickest to spot the hidden traps. We survive by mobilizing our paranoia, living with worst-case assumptions.

Realistically, we have to face the question 'What else can we do?' If we love our neighbour and drop our guard, the chances are that he or she will exploit us. To be exploited is to be proved a fool and lowers our self-esteem. The cost of this prevailing attitude is that we live in an angry and divided society where violence is an increasing part of our way of life. The people who are unheard learn that they must batter their way into a position of power. Hence the growing violence among the oppressed in South Africa, Palestine, Sri Lanka. It is closest to ourselves in Northern Ireland; it lurks as an option wherever rulers refuse to listen. The marginalized are quick to seize whatever will gain them a hearing, whether it is a bomb, a missile launcher or a gun to hijack a plane. Long ago a psychiatrist coined the phrase 'It's better to be wanted for murder than not to be wanted at all'.

So what has all this to say about the Church, its leadership, morale and mission? When we adopt the style of the times and forget the essential insights of the gospel, we become part of the spiral of aggression. We then validate the general attitude by our example: 'Look the church is doing it, it must be all right.' Misusing the Bible, we provide a theology which justifies bitter political struggle, the devaluing of opponents, the marginalizing of those that we have managed to outvote. There are texts which on their own seem to allow witch-hunts, but only at the expense of forgetting the personality of Jesus and the way in which he treated the outsider and the marginalized. Simon Barrington Ward, when he was general secretary of CMS, wrote about the Church as the 'fellowship of the unlike'. At the moment we seem tempted to gather under party labels which define our theological membership, our sexual orientation or our political attitudes and then we exclude those who do not share them.

It is no coincidence, I fear, that the scurrilous behaviour of one newspaper with a supposed mission to expose 'gay vicars' was linked in time with the apparently high-minded, biblically-based debate in the General Synod of the Church of England about sexual morality. It was the same paper which unearthed the story of Lambeth's attempts to secure Terry Waite's release. Immediately the culture of suspicion gets to work: 'Who has got it in for whom, behind what front?' The spirit of Jesus becomes submerged in a political game played in the name of Christianity.

How does this picture of confused authority and low morale lead us to any insight about Mission?

I have tried to demonstrate a connection between the problems within the life of the Church and those of the world around. As Christians we are sharing the dilemmas and trying some of the unhelpful solutions of the secular world. We are aware of the way that they are at variance with the gospel command to love one another.

What we have to offer the world in its search for a new society is repentance for the way that we are behaving in the Church. At every level, from congregation, through diocese and province, to the Lambeth Conference, we have to go back to the experience of Christians who have struggled to live by the mind of the crucified. The New Testament phrases crowd in: 'Love your neighbour'; 'Do good to them that persecute you'; 'Do nothing from selfishness or conceit but in humility count others better than yourselves'; 'Love is never jealous: love is not boastful or conceited . . . it never seeks its own advantage, it does not take offence or store up grievances.'

By adopting the political responses of secular society, we appear to sanctify them. Yet this is no way for human beings to live; it is becoming clear as well that this is not even a way for the human race to survive in a nuclear age.

The Church's mission is to take seriously the life and teaching of Jesus and translate it into our own structures. We have to risk the vulnerability of authority. We have to learn to say 'yes' to the people who appear to cut across our path and to find a way of including their talents within the whole. We have to avoid the manipulative techniques which threaten to walk out if we do not get our way. We have to avoid pushing people out who we find too difficult.

Humanity is in a crisis of power and authority. A church which can demonstrate a way of living in community has a real message of hope for the world. Alongside our many other tasks, I believe therefore that we need to take very seriously our own situation and begin where we are, with ourselves. Let us look at what is happening in the vestry, in the diocese, in the ecumenical relations in our town and begin to do something about them. No one person is going to solve the nation's problems, let alone the world's, but if each of us in our own sphere begins to explore the possibility of new relationships, there are enough of us working together to point to a hope of salvation that could run round the globe.

The Christian ministry today swings uncomfortably between the two poles of authority and service. 'Why doesn't the bishop give a lead?' is an antiphon sung in counterpoint to the complaint, 'He ought to listen to us and let the parish set its own agenda'. Any attempt at Provincial strategy is met with the complaint against policy-makers: 'They are there to serve the dioceses, not try to tell us what to do.' Ordinands trained for the stipendiary ministry find themselves crammed full of liturgical scholarship only to encounter the brigadier who says: 'Don't muck about with our prayer book, padre.'

One can only guess that these problems were felt as much in the early church as they have been in the succeeding Christian generations. Why else would the gospels associate the eucharist with stories of self-assertion and teaching about self-abasement?

Luke's gospel is particulary strong on this. It is he who reports the power struggle at the Passover supper. Mark and Matthew tie it up with the ambitious hopes of James and John, but keep the Passion/eucharistic reference in Jesus' reply: 'Can you drink the cup that I am going to drink?' (Mark 10: 35–45; Matt. 20: 20–28) If we are right in thinking that the author was an intimate of St. Paul, perhaps it was a theme particularly relevant to somebody who had suffered in the company of that most autocratic of humble men. All the Synoptists repeat the theme on the occasion when Jesus sits the child in the midst. St. John picks up the teaching and gives it visual form in the feet-washing. This adds a baptismal reference, so perhaps it is something that every Christian has to struggle with and not just the ordained. It is part of the lesson that we have to learn if we are washed into participation in the life of Christ.

The church has its traditional disciples, the daily office among them. Who says how these are to be observed? Who might have the power to accept variants? How does the person to whom in one form or another the words have been said 'Take thou authority' tell those who disagree that they are wrong without sounding arrogant? One way out of the dilemma is to suggest that one 'does what Jesus did'. But that is actually a cop-out, leaving the matter to private judgement and diminishing the corporate understanding of the Church. Besides, a sentimental claim that I am washing somebody's feet wears thin when it is observed that I am doing it by kneeling on the toes of at least two others. It is easy enough to observe that authority can topple over into arrogance and that servanthood without discipline becomes sloppiness. But what are we going to do about it?

Those who have thought about this subject may think that they see where I am heading. This is the point at which I produce the joker in the pack 'accountability' and cut the knot by subjecting authority to the scrutiny of others. At the other end servanthood and supervision also go together, so demands can be monitored and the compulsive desire to be on one's knees scrubbing dirty toenails can be questioned. This is a sensible attempt to bring secular insight to bear on the extremes of ecclesiastical pathology. I would not deny that there is much to be learned from organizational theory about how things could be managed better. It could be drawn neatly on a chart and if there were the equipment here to do it I'd be the first to try my hand. But in fact, instructive as it is, nobody lives on a chart. The clinically neat design is never replicated in real life. The people you try to be accountable to are irresponsibly tainted with their own prejudices. The supervisor's quick appraisal of your distorted perceptions are partly true and partly a function of his or her own bias. Human variables make it difficult to deliver what is required. In addition, the complexity of real life demands that the design stand out in 3D. A flat chart with its neat line shows one area of accountability. In experience we are accountable to a number of different groups and the areas all overlap. It can be distracting and painful to be caught in the different circles of accountability.

In the course of our pilgrimage we grow and learn, but one of the things we learn is that the idea that we can be universally loved or always right is part of our infantile fantasy. We have to accept the gifts and the failures, the adequacy and the inadequacy that make up all of us. Until we have done this we are not only difficult people to live with, but also psychologically dangerous. If we cannot bear our own inadequacies, then we will deny them and spend our time finding fault, sometimes quite maliciously, with others.

There are few things calculated to make you feel better and more virtuous than stoning an adulteress. That however is a luxury most of us are denied. Instead we make do with pillorying the small faults of others. The more obsessed we get with them, the more we need to look at ourselves and see what is going on.

Which brings me back to the place at which I started, the dilemma of human relationships as we break the bread. The divisions among Christians, fuelled mostly by their unacknowledged needs for status and acceptance, love and power, have been the scandal which have turned people back from the gospel, whether in the local church life at Corinth, in the power-hungry politics of the medieval church, in the bitterness of the Reformation or the divisions of denominations since. Christians have an astonishing ability to be beastly to each other in the name of the God of love.

The disciples, as they gathered for the meal, wanted to find out who was top. They wanted to know who would win the debate about the ordination of women or the right way to run a decade of evangelism. What they got was authoritative rebuke and loving acceptance and perhaps at the time they did not appreciate either. St. John's version has a very human note when Peter says to the

Lord, 'Not my feet. I'm the Prince of humble men. You've got it wrong!' In the short term he was expressing something for all of us because the most perfect love and the most generous authority can feel like a threat. We pull back, we test it out, we ask for it all to happen in a more manageable way. So however much we dream of it, there is never going to be a church where there is no conflict, tension, resentment. We ourselves act out of our part-healed personalities and what we offer is received or rejected by equally damaged persons who cloud the present with past misunderstanding. The struggle is built in and is to be accepted as the way that we grow, not by defeating those with whom we disagree, but by learning about ourselves through interaction with them. To make that possible is the service offered by a wise authority.

# Chapter 9

# The Emotional Costs of Caring

Richard Holloway

*Richard Holloway is Bishop of Edinburgh in the Scottish Episcopal Church, a much respected figure within the Church of England and a regular contributor to the* Church Times. *He was raised in the Vale of Leven and after ministries in Glasgow's Gorbals and Edinburgh's Royal Mile, he went to Boston USA, the city in which he met his wife while at Harvard. He returned to Edinburgh via a chaplaincy in Oxford. His gaunt, crew-cut figure belies his warmth and twinkling humour, but betrays his love of high-church ritual. However, his vision is broad and he is a leading proponent of women's ordination within the high-church party. Richard Holloway's many books are a record of his pilgrimage through various theological enthusiasms, but throughout them all his sensitivity towards human nature has earthed his thinking, as in this contribution on the role of the carer delivered as an address to social workers.*

There is an ancient and important philosophical distinction between grounds and causes for an action. The best way to explain the distinction is to give an example. It comes from a recent biography of C. S. Lewis by A. N. Wilson, and I use it simply to illustrate the point, not to agree or disagree with the view expressed by Wilson.

    C. S. Lewis was converted to Christianity while he was a Don at Oxford. The grounds of his conversion, the reasons he gave for it, were first that he had become intellectually persuaded that there was a God; and, secondly, that God had come into history in the person of Jesus Christ. These were the grounds, the reasons, he gave for his conversion, but A. N. Wilson suggests another cause. At the time of his conversion Lewis lived with the mother of a man he had befriended in the army during the First World War and whom he had promised to take care of. Wilson believes that C. S. Lewis and Mrs Moore had had a sexual relationship which was becoming increasingly difficult for Lewis to sustain. By becoming a Christian, Wilson implies, Lewis would be given the perfect way out of an aspect of the relationship that had become a burden to him, and this, probably unconscious motive, was the secret cause of his conversion. The ground, then, is the reason we give for an action, while the cause is what actually makes it happen. I suspect that most human action is a combination of rational grounds and psychological or practical causes, though each case will differ according to the circumstances. This distinction points to the ambiguity in any human undertaking. There is always a sub-text, always a mixture of motive.

However, there are determinists who would claim that there is never any validity in the grounds offered for an action, except as a way of achieving intellectual respectability for something that is done for other reasons. Psychologists call this rationalizing, finding reasons or grounds for conduct actually motivated by other causes. The trouble with deterministic theories of any sort is that they are all circular and ultimately self-defeating. If everything is determined, then the doctrine that everything is determined is itself determined, so how can we rationally evaluate it? One approach to caring would be deterministic. It would claim that the emotional cost of caring is precisely what attracts people to the work in the first place. They would claim that the principle that determines all human activity is pleasure or self-satisfaction. People get into the situations they get into because they want to, and what attracts people to caring is precisely the stress associated with it, the cost of it. Remove it and your remove the motivation, take the fun out of it. Carers are stress junkies, people who need to be needed. To take the costing out of caring for them is like taking the pain out of masochism for masochists. Do that and you remove the point of the activity.

Now there probably are people of whom this could be said. If you did a personality profile on them you would discover that they derive their identity, their sense of themselves, their validation, by caring for others. They need to be needed. Wherever the need comes from, it is clearly beneficial to society, which exploits it with a vengeance. Carers of this sort collude with the exploitation. Warning them against burn-out is like telling Olympic sprinters to take it easy. Burn-out is what it is all about. Some of the most effective and magnificent carers in history have been people like this. They burn with an intense white flame and consume themselves in the process. The problems presented by white-hot carers to the managers of the institutions in which they operate are complex, but I'll note only two aspects in passing: their tendency to make a universal paradigm out of their own psychological intensity – everyone has to do it like them; and the second problem is what to do with them in their middle age when they are, in fact, burned out. Middle-aged emotional veterans are a problem for any organization that is not able to pension them off handsomely, but it is not one I want to spend any time on today, though it is a crucially important topic. These are the unmanageable carers, either through holiness or pathology. They streak like meteors and are gone, leaving the rest of us to handle the impossible expectations they have aroused.

But what about the less intense, more straightforward people in the caring professions, the people who are not stress junkies. Let me attempt a classification of stress among carers, since stress is the currency in question. I'd like to suggest seven elements.

The first reminds me of words they shouted at Jesus on the cross: 'He saved others. Himself he cannot save.' It has frequently been observed that professional carers are often bad at owning their own needs. In many of them there is a kind of minor Messianic complex, a need to be terrific all the time, to appear to be invulnerable. Today we distrust that complex, we recognize the importance of failure, what they call the wounded surgeon phenomenon, after T. S. Eliot's

> The wounded surgeon plies the steel
> that questions the distempered part.
> Beneath the bleeding hands we feel
> the sharp compassion of the healer's art.

One of the best modern therapeutic insights is that the wounded make the best healers. This is the abiding contribution that Alcoholics Anonymous has made to the human sciences. There is a solidarity in weakness, shared weakness can achieve strength. Examples of the wounded healer phenomenon increase daily, especially in the USA where new obsessions and social and personal pathologies seem to multiply like weeds, and alongside them spring up recovery groups tailored to every type of compulsion. I had a friend in Boston who belonged to Alcoholics Anonymous, Alanon, Sex Addicts Anonymous, Food Bingers Anonymous, Destructive Relationships Anonymous, and one or two others. She got so addicted to recovery groups that she is now working on a group to get people off going to groups – so far they have not been able to find a free night.

A recent development in this area was provided by the Grassmarket Project in Edinburgh which mounted a play by homeless men about their lives in the lodging house and night shelter. Under the direction of Jeremy Weller the play *Glad* was a sell-out and has since played in London and Berlin, and will soon open in Glasgow. Meanwhile the company is working on a new play, *Bad*, using boys in Polmont Borstal and plans a third play called *Mad*, about the mentally ill. It has been extraordinarily taxing for these young theatre producers to be permanently immersed in the violent and chaotic world of the homeless at that level, and only recently has some support structure been offered.

This work and much of the work done in the field of HIV is performed by untrained carers, who soon fall victim to stress. HIV is a good example of both sides of this phenomenon. Much of the cost of HIV/AIDS is borne by women, ill-equipped for the task and likely to be affected personally by the virus, or through their partners, parents, siblings. Much emphasis is laid by society on the importance of such informal care, but it brings enormous costs upon the carers, who are also likely to be battling against a syndrome of stress from poverty, illness and poor housing.

The problem with applying the wounded surgeon thesis to HIV/ AIDS is that we are essentially managing an intractable condition, so the optimism, the hope of recovery that can energize participants in other programmes is a scarcer commodity.

What all these groups show us is the importance of congruence, emotional and psychological continuity between the carer and the cared for. Unflawed healers, untroubled carers patronize and depress us with their own apparent invulnerability. They need to learn how to acknowledge their own weaknesses and needs, if only because failure to acknowledge them will damage their sensitivity and effectiveness, and create a delusionary self-image. The need to appear to be without problems is itself a source of stress. This is a particular issue among clergy who are supposed to be invulnerable to all the normal human passions and doubts. Some of them think they are, of course, and they become useless at real caring. Owning up can be a relief, just like coming out of the other closets in which we hide. Systems of pastoring and support need to be set up for carers, though they may not be at their most effective if they are within the employing organization. This, again, is an insight that informs the best in current practice.

Statutory organizations and larger voluntary organizations are often quite good at producing the kind of support systems that enable carers to share the complex issues that face them. But what about carers in small voluntary organizations, especially in the field of HIV/AIDS? Would it not be possible for local authorities and larger, more established voluntary organizations to assist these nickel-and-dime operations by seconding workers to them skilled in the areas they lack? Secondment of skilled administrators and support staff would provide stability, enabling the small organizations to do what they do best, which is to support and speak for HIV individuals and families. The cost of secondment as opposed to grant-aid might be a better use of scarce resources.

Apart from the importance of acknowledging their own fears and anxieties, professional carers have to learn to live with the almost impossible tension created by the fact that they are information receivers, people who encourage others to talk and face the reality of their situation, and yet they also have power over the lives of their informants and may have to act on information received in favoured and confessional circumstances. This second source of stress is a particularly cruel dilemma for the statutory social worker, productive of enormous stress and guilt.

Thirdly, caring for others, especially the vulnerable or chronically dependent, is radically devitalizing. The heart of the problem lies in the intractability of many of the problems carers confront, leading to the treadmill effect. How do you measure success in sweeping back the tide? Enough can never be done, and recognizing that fact can afflict the carer with a desperate compulsiveness that is highly destructive. Carers have to learn the very difficult lesson of detachment, a balance between proper involvement and personal survival. They are not responsible for the universe. They have to learn that it is all right to need a break, to have had enough, to walk away.

The fourth type of stress I call contingent stress, because it comes from being answerable to social and political structures. This is a potent source of stress at the moment in dealing with children's issues. Related to it is the frontier area between caring (the primary object and what carers' drives and training are for) and the secondary, adversative consequences of the primary purpose. For example, in order to care for the child the parent may have to be prosecuted. It is unlikely that the same person will always have the emotional and intellectual complexity required for both sides of that exercise. Social workers are not well equipped to be prosecutors, yet contemporary social structures increasingly impose duties upon them for which they are rarely prepared by training or temperament, giving rise to an enormous source of stress. How one might begin to separate these two functions I do not know. I am increasingly persuaded that we ask of social workers a combination of attributes that is almost impossible to achieve: compassion and pragmatic discernment, the psychic tug-of-war between their commitment to their clients and their responsibility to society.

A fifth type of stress, and one that is related to the previous type, is cognitive stress produced by the knowledge explosion. What is real knowledge in the field of human caring and human abuse? We know how cognitive systems change in all disciplines. (Once upon a time they kept you in bed for two weeks after an appendix operation; now they have you running round the hospital grounds within twenty-four hours.) During periods of transition in knowledge systems there is intense pressure upon practitioners, some of whom are scrupulously anxious to respond to new knowledge and feel intellectually displaced a lot of the time. Others enter recurrent phases of defensive stress, because they believed profoundly in the defeated systems and new knowledge is endlessly resisted. Since no one ever blows a whistle and calls a break in the evolution of knowledge, people in the field get very battered indeed.

Perhaps the most contentious example of contemporary cognitive stress is provided by the new reproductive techniques that permit children to be conceived by donor insemination from an anonymous father (AID), whose perpetual anonymity is protected by current legislation. Even more radical are the techniques for embryo implantation, whereby the resulting child will have two legal parents and two genetic parents. A recent complicating element was distractingly added by the so-called Virgin Birth case.

People instinctively take sides on these issues. From the point of view of this chapter, the stress comes in evaluating the rights of the infertile when they seem to counter the rights of the child. AID has been used for several decades and we know the effect it can have on donor offspring when they are told they may not be given more than general details about their genetic fathers. Make full disclosure compulsory, the clinicians tell us, and the number of men prepared to donate sperm will be reduced to next to nothing. I'm not taking sides in this debate here, but it does provide us with a good example of cognitive stress.

The sixth type is political stress and it comes in various forms. Directors of social work know all about budget struggles and the political in-fighting that characterizes them, especially in relations with the voluntary sector. But the type of political stress I really want to note comes from the social and political context of human need. Carers often see themselves as professional palliators of systematic evils, who are cynically exploited by the system. For instance, those who care for homeless teenagers can be intensely frustrated by a society that creates the problem in the first place and then refuses to provide adequate means to palliate it. Such carers are likely to become politically committed, however privately, and this can add its own stress in the professional context, especially in areas of political sensitivity and social volatility. Many carers feel like garbage operatives in a throw-away society.

Carers on the ragged edge of social policy as it effects immigrants, for instance, or carers of the mentally ill, as society moves officially away from institutionalization to care in the community, can be very conflicted in their attitude to government. There is nothing more morally destructive than being among the front-line troops in a war you don't quite believe in. It is not surprising that many social workers feel as unloved as the poor, bloody infantry.

Finally, we have to note that carers, especially professional carers, are increasingly used by society as official scapegoats for intractable social problems. If you are trying to set up an AIDS facility you will become the target for vituperative abuse from the 'not in my backyard' brigade. Even more notoriously, if you are a social worker engaged with the complex phenomenon of child abuse, you are likely to become the focus of society's intense frustration at being unable to respond neatly to such a complex evil.

What, for instance, do you do if you are working with chronic sex offenders, when you know there is only one unit in the country that is trying to rehabilitate them? You begin to feel more like a transportation officer than a social worker, a ritual element in the deadly switchback of offence, arrest, imprisonment, release – re-offence, re-arrest and so on for ever.

How do you handle the phenomenon, not of seedy and solitary sex offenders, but the network of allegedly organized child abusers, ritualized or not? A horrendously complex and inexact phenomenon in itself, it is made a hundred times worse by the obsessive attention of the press and broadcasting media. Their tendency is to create stories in order to be able to report them, or, by the manner of their reporting, to make it almost impossible to arrive at an objective judgement.

Cumulatively, these types of stress add up to a high emotional cost. How do we handle it? In conclusion I'd like to suggest three simple axioms. First of all, carers should prepare for stress the way riot police prepare for public abuse. Carers should know that stress comes with the territory. Knowing in advance won't take the pain out of it, but it might take away some of the surprise. Secondly, knowing that you will never eradicate it, learn how to manage it through a combination of personal and group techniques. Social work departments should set up groups called 'Stressees Anonymous', in which carers can swop war stories and achieve the mysterious grace that comes from solidarity in weakness. Finally, accept that stress is intrinsic to the job and don't get into it if you can't cope. Instead, go off and become a Borders shepherd.

# Chapter 10

# Defending the Faith: Militant Protestantism in Modern Scotland

Steve Bruce

*Steve Bruce is Professor of Sociology in the University of Aberdeen. He was educated at the University of Stirling then taught at Queen's University, Belfast. His speciality is the sociology of religion. A non-believer, he has brought objectivity and fairness to his studies of militant Protestantism in Scotland and Northern Ireland which have become the definitive books on the subject while remaining accessible to the general reader. One of the puzzles of Scottish religious life this century is not the existence of sectarianism but why it has not gained ground apace with events in Northern Ireland. (Most of the Ulster Protestants originated in Scotland, and most of the Roman Catholics in the west of Scotland originated in Ireland.) Steve Bruce helps us to see why, in this contribution which is reprinted from* Scotia the American-Canadian Journal of Scottish studies.

There are a number of superficial similarities between the sectarian conflict of Ulster and the relations between Protestants and Catholics in Scotland. The Presbyterians of Ulster are descended from their Scottish co-religionists and there are close ties between the churches. The Catholic population of Scotland is largely a product of Irish migration. Ease of movement and close family ties have ensured that the recent civil unrest in Northern Ireland has produced a response in western and central Scotland. The streets of Glasgow have been the scene for clashes between IRA sympathizers and Scottish Loyalists.

Yet for all the similarities it is obvious that Protestant-Catholic relations do not have the importance in Scotland that they have in Ulster. Religious identity does not have the saliency for the Scots that it has for the people of Northern Ireland. This chapter is concerned to gauge and document militant Protestantism in Scotland and, by comparison with Ulster, to identify the structural features that permit or retard secularization. The ways in which secularization undermines militant Protestantism will then be examined and finally, the problems caused for remaining militant Protestants by the fragmentation of religious and political Protestantism are discussed.

The Roman Catholic population of modern Scotland has two quite distinct parts: that which is descended from the Scottish Highland Catholics and that descended from Irish immigrants. Although Scotland is usually thought of as an especially Protestant country, the Reformation was by no means complete. Small pockets of Roman Catholicism remained and inadequate provision of ministers by the Presbyterian Church left a vacuum which was filled by Roman Catholic priests. Thus, in the remoter parts of the Highlands and Islands, and in parts of the north-east, enclaves of Catholicism remained. South of the Highland line, however, Roman Catholics could be numbered in hundreds: Bishop Hay's census in 1780 claimed only 6,600.

The position changed drastically at the end of the eighteenth and beginning of the nineteenth century. The growth of industry in the western and central lowlands was the 'pull' factor, and the failure of the 1798 rebellion and the famines were the 'push' that led to large-scale Irish immigration. In 1795 there were only fifty Catholics in Glasgow; by 1829 there were 25,000. Edinburgh in 1829 had about 14,000 Catholics; thirty years earlier there had been fewer than a thousand. Economic and social change and a failed rebellion also persuaded people to leave the Highlands. This migration meant that a small part of the Roman Catholic population of industrial Scotland would have been native Scottish.

Not all of the Irish immigrants were Roman Catholics. Some of them were Protestants and, significantly, members of the Episcopal Church of Ireland. The denomination is important because in the eighteenth and early nineteenth century organized anti-Catholicism was generally a Church of Ireland phenomenon. The Ulster Presbyterians were still occasionally flirting with republicanism in the form of the United Irishmen and being discriminated against by the Episcopal gentry.

The arrival of the Irish in Scotland not only introduced the basic material for anti-Catholicism – a large number of Catholics – but it also brought a group of Protestants who were already militantly anti-Catholic. These Orangemen were responsible for the first recorded Orange Walks in Scotland, in 1821 and 1822.

Most commentators note that there was little or no sectarian bitterness in the Highlands and Islands. Even where the evangelical revival had its greatest impact and theological argument was at its most violent, actual social relations were quite amicable. This may have resulted, as Drummond and Bulloch suggest (in *The Church in Victorian Scotland, 1843–1874*), from the fairly 'Protestant' character of Highland Catholics, whose close proximity to Calvinists seems to have produced a Jansenist seriousness that distinguished them from

Irish Catholics. Ayrshire and Lanarkshire, however, provided a quite different picture. The classic combination of an alien ethnic minority, identified by a distinct language, possessing the religion that Scottish Protestantism was formed to oppose, competing with the indigenous working class for the same resources, produced fairly regular but minor disorders and public disturbances.

Protestant churchmen did something to fuel the conflict. The various public events that signalled the increasing acceptance of Roman Catholics – the Emancipation Act (1832), government grant to the Roman Catholic Maynooth college (1845), the restoration of first the English (1850) and then the Scottish Roman Catholic Church hierarchies (1878) – were greeted with predictable hostility by some church leaders. Societies such as the Scottish Reformation Society and the Scottish Protestant Association were formed and anti-Catholic journals were launched. A leading Free Church minister, James Begg of Newington, sponsored a charlatan named Patrick McMenemy who claimed to have been a Catholic priest and gave public displays of the blasphemous mass for the entertainment and outrage of Protestants. A literature of tales of violated nuns and depraved priests became popular. None the less, it is an unenthusiastic anti-Catholicism one finds in the main Protestant churches. The Church of Scotland in particular was no great supporter of militant Protestantism. Even among Free Church ministers, anti-Catholicism did not loom large in their interests. In one collection of biographical sketches of seventy prominent Free Church leaders, only four individuals are identified with anti-Catholic activities. Of course, anti-popery was so much taken for granted in Victorian Protestantism in Scotland that we cannot infer from their lack of active involvement any great sympathy for the Roman Catholic faith. None the less, it remains significant that few Protestant ministers actively engaged in anti-Catholic propaganda (almost certainly because the energy of the controversialists was directed primarily to the great internal Presbyterian squabbles).

There was a distinct increase in anti-Catholic feeling in the 1920s and '30s which had its origins in resentment at the Irish Nationalists taking advantage of Britain's involvement in the First World War, and in a feeling that the 1918 Education Act had, in the words of a writer in the *United Free Church Record* in 1924, given 'enormous and unfair privileges' to the separate Roman Catholic schools. Protestant political parties had some success with Alexander Ratcliffe and the Scottish Protestant League taking seats in the Glasgow Corporation and John Cormack of the Protestant Action Society being elected for the Leith Ward in Edinburgh. Support for these parties died before or during the Second World War and while Cormack continued to hold the Leith seat until the 1960s, it was his personal reputation as an Independent rather than his militant Protestantism that people voted for. When he died, the support also died.

The Orange Order is today the main organizational form for anti-Catholicism in Scotland. Quite how many Orangemen there are is a matter of conjecture; the leadership generally claim 80,000 but a figure of between 40,000 and 50,000 would be nearer the total number who turn out for the annual Orange Walk. Equally difficult to gauge is the nature of the motivation to be an Orangeman. Although the constitution of the organization still uses the language of evangelical Protestantism, it is obvious that the vast majority of the members are not 'born-again' Christians. Members are expected to be members of a Protestant denomination, but even this is obviously not enforced.

To the 'right' of the Orange Order is a group called the Scottish Loyalists. Mostly young Orangemen, the Loyalists formed in 1979 to oppose, with violence if necessary, the marches organized in Glasgow to support various Irish republican causes such as the Troops Out movement and the Hunger Strike committee. Although the core of the Scottish Loyalists numbers only around a hundred, marches and demonstrations during the lead-up to the Pope's visit to Glasgow drew crowds of up to four thousand.

There are also in Scotland branches of the Apprentice Boys of Derry (with perhaps a thousand members) and groups related to the paramilitary Ulster Defence Association and Ulster Volunteer Force. The UDA and UVF have always been numerically insignificant in Scotland, but they do have some importance in their ability to embarrass the leadership of the Orange Order and to undermine the respectable image of other militant Protestants.

The above organizations make up what, for convenience, I will call secular Protestantism. The attitude of the main Protestant churches in Scotland towards Roman Catholicism can be briefly described as follows. The Church of Scotland, the United Free Church, the Episcopal Church in Scotland, and the Methodists, Baptists and Congregationalists tend to a liberal and ecumenical view which accepts the right of Roman Catholics to enjoy the same privileges as other Christian believers. The conservative Protestant churches – the Free Church and the Free Presbyterian Church – remain committed to the traditional theology of the Westminster Confession and its judgement of the Pope as the 'anti-christ', but these two bodies draw most of their support from the Highlands and Islands of Scotland and thus have little overlap with the areas in which the Orange Order and the other militant Protestant organizations are at their strongest.

The secular Protestant organizations in Scotland all have counterparts in Ulster, as do the Protestant churches. As the main concern of this chapter is comparison, attention will now be given to the career of Pastor Jack Glass, who has attempted to create and mobilize in Scotland a religio-political movement similar to Ulster's Paisley-ism. While most of frequent press identifications of Glass as 'Scot-land's Ian Paisley' are superficial in the extreme, the comparison of the two Protestant leaders, who embody the synthesis of politics and theology that is at the heart of anti-Catholicism, seems likely to illustrate the potential that Ulster and Scotland have for militant Protestantism. If it seems a little inappropriate in an essay concerned with broad social tendencies to concentrate on one individual, then the major point has been missed. That the career of Glass is the main point of purchase on Scottish militant Protestantism is itself a result of the secularization that has affected Scotland considerably more than it has Ulster, a point that will be pursued later.

Glass was raised in a working-class home in Paisley, Ayrshire. His parents were both evangelical Christians and he was converted in a Salvation Army Sunday School. During his period of national service, Glass became influenced by the teachings of Dr Martyn Lloyd-Jones, the Welsh Calvinist pastor of Westminster Chapel, London. His newly-acquired commitment to Calvinism – the doc-trines of 'sovereign grace' – was wedded to a Baptist belief in the necessity for adult or believer's (rather than infant) baptism. This caused a problem with church affiliation. The Scottish Protestant churches that remain Calvinist (the two Free Churches) are Presby-terian and hold to infant baptism; the Baptist Church is not Calvinist. Glass solved the problem by training at the Free Church College as a private student and then beginning an independent ministry in Glasgow in what he rather clumsily named the Zion Sovereign Grace Evangelical Baptist Church.

What distinguishes Glass from other theologically conservative Protestants in Scotland is his willingness to make public protests against things which offend his religion and morality. He has regu-larly picked ecumenical gatherings and meetings addressed by Church of Scotland clergy who have met the Pope.

Glass first met Ian Paisley in the early 1960s when he invited him to preach in Glasgow. Their first joint ventures were religious rather than expressly political; going to Rome together to protest at the Archbishop of Canterbury meeting the Pope, for example. With the start of the present period of civil unrest in Ulster, Glass became more involved in explicitly political demonstrations and in 1970 he, Ian Paisley and Brian Green, a Strict Baptist preacher in London, all stood for Parliament. Paisley was returned for North Antrim. Glass and Green polled very badly.

Glass has gradually built his church up to three congregations; his own in Polmadie, Glasgow, and two others in Dumfries and Kilmarnock. He formed the Twentieth Century Reformation

Movement to act as a vehicle for his political activity and for his social and moral crusades but it has never grown beyond the limits of his church membership. In the late 1960s, Glass, in his own words, 'separated from Ian Paisley' because of the latter's association with the American fundamentalist Bob Jones. Glass felt that the true Calvinist should renounce the Arminian errors of the American fundamentalist tradition. Paisley continued to claim to be both a Calvinist *and* a fundamentalist.

The planned papal visit to Scotland in 1982 (the first time a Pope visited Scotland) caused Glass to contest two elections on a 'Protestant Crusade Against the Papal Visit' ticket. The first, a by-election in Hillhead, provided Glass with excellent publicity as the seat was also contested (and won) by the Rt Hon Roy Jenkins, one of the founders of the Social Democratic Party. A month later he contested the local government elections for the ward, Bellahouston, where the papal mass had been held. The results of Glass's three elections are given in Table 1.

The Hillhead by-election stands out from the others as a particularly poor result but the constituency takes in the university area, is heavily middle class and, although he lives there, was always an unlikely place for Glass to poll well. In his own words, 'the Hillhead constituency is professional cum academic and in religious terms, ecumenical and romanising'. Bridgeton and Bellahouston both have a considerable working-class constituency, and in both elections Glass got around 7 per cent of the vote and almost matched the Scottish Nationalist Party candidate. In both cases the Labour candidate was comfortably returned.

Glass's Percentage Vote

| Bridgeton Gen. Election June 1970 | Hillhead By-election March 1982 | Bellahouston District Council July 1982 |
|---|---|---|
| Lab. 65.5 | SDP. 33.4 | Lab. 41.2 |
| Con. 18.3 | Con. 26.7 | Con. 23.8 |
| SNP. 9.2 | Lab. 25.9 | SDP. 21.3 |
| Glass 7.0 | SNP. 11.3 | SNP. 7.1 |
|  | Glass 1.3 | Glass 6.7 |
| TOTAL 16,867 | 30,289 | 8,020 |

The only other recent occasion on which candidates have stood on a Protestant ticket was at the local elections in Edinburgh in June 1982. Twelve people, led by Jim Maclean, the secretary of the Edinburgh Loyalist Coalition,* stood on a 'Protestant Crusade Against the Papal Visit' platform in the Lothian regional elections. Their best poll was 170 votes.

The contrast with Ulster can be starkly made by noting that Ian Paisley's Free Presbyterian Church, founded a decade earlier than Glass's body, now has over 10,000 members in fifty-two congregations. Paisley's political career has been no less successful. In the first three direct elections for the European Assembly, Paisley gained more first preference votes than any other candidate. The Democratic Unionist Party has three of the seventeen Ulster seats at the Westminster Parliament and rivals the Official Unionist Party as the main representative of Ulster Unionism.

Given the importance of the papacy as a symbol for Protestants of the error of Romanism, one would expect that the reactions to the Pope's visit to Scotland would be a good gauge of the strength of anti-Catholicism. The announcement of the visit brought forth petitions and demonstrations but, in the event, the predictions of major civil disturbance proved to be grossly exaggerated. The largest protest on the day was one organized by the Scottish Loyalists with around four thousand marchers. The meeting which was supposed to be the climax to the protests, called by the Orange Order in the centre of Glasgow, and addressed by the Grand Master of the Order and Ian Paisley, drew fewer than one thousand people, and most of those were the young Scottish Loyalists whom the leadership of the Orange Order had condemned as 'young drunk rowdies'.

Although the various Protestant groups lay the blame for the lack of protest at different doors, there is general agreement that the campaign had been a failure. The evangelical Protestants blame the secular Protestants. Glass's view is that: 'The only people who were in the front line were people from Paisley's church, my own church and the Jock Troup Memorial. You had about 300 born-again Bible Protestants and your 80,000 Orangemen were not to be seen.' The militant secular Protestants in the Scottish Loyalists blame the failure on the leadership of the Orange Order who, they believe, should have been more aggressively militant. The Orange Order blame the failure on the militants for discrediting the protest. While a number of incidental factors are relevant – the Falklands war upstaged the papal visit, and the campaign lost a lot of its momentum in the weeks immediately before the visit when it was expected to be cancelled – the general lack of militant Protestant reaction can be

---

*The coalition involves the Scottish Protestant Union, the Protestant Action Society and the Apprentice Boys of Derry. The Orange Order does not, as a body, join any coalitions, but the above organizations are basically composed of the same small number of people and they are all Orangemen.

taken as a reasonable reflection of the state of anti-Catholicism in Scotland.

In the remainder of this chapter various structural features which have undermined anti-Catholicism will be analysed, and the crisis of motivation that such undermining presents for the remaining militant Protestants will be examined.

The paradigmatic case for religio-political conflict occurs when most sections of a society identify themselves by contrast with a readily identifiable threatening group and use their religious affiliation as a major part of that identity. In such a case, the clergy act as legitimators for the conflict (although as members of the intellectual professional class they are vulnerable to modernizing and secularizing influences). This is the case in Ulster and South Africa, and in the southern states of America in the last century and the early part of this century. It is not, however, the case in Scotland, and I will now examine some of the crucial ways in which Scotland differs from Ulster.

In the first place, Scottish Catholics are Scottish. They do not have the option of adopting an alternative national identity. There is no surrounding state to which they can claim allegiance. Where the Catholics of Ulster can think of themselves as citizens of the Irish Republic (and symbolize that commitment by drawing Eire passports), the Catholics in Scotland have no option other than to be Scottish or British. The difference this makes in terms of the threat posed to Scottish Protestants can be clearly seen in the nature of what the Protestant mythology portrays as the aim of the Catholics. For Ulster Protestants, the end of Catholic action is the dissolution of Ulster as a political entity and the destruction of 'the Protestant way of life'. This can be seen as a fairly tangible aim which *could* easily be accomplished. The Scottish Orange mythology cannot suppose that the Scottish Catholics are likely to drag Scotland into a political entity with a strong Catholic identity; there is no such state available, and so the perceived threat to Scottish Protestants is the much weaker one of internal subversion. Orange leaders believe that Roman Catholics are assiduously altering the nature of life in Scotland (and Great Britain) and undermining Protestantism in the eventual hope of creating a world-wide dictatorship of Rome. This threat is either implausible or, if one can believe in it at all, too distant to provoke widespread anxiety. The position of Catholics in Scotland does not allow for the creation of a plausible and serious threat.

Related to this point is the question of scale and encirclement. Ulster Protestants are encircled by Catholicism; they have nowhere else to go. Whereas the threat *pervades* Ulster, it is *localized* in Scotland. While theologically conservative Protestants in the north of Scotland may share a dislike for the religious teachings of Roman

Catholicism, they are not actually confronted by sizeable Catholic populations. While Scottish Protestants in Lanark and Ayrshire may feel their ethnic identity under threat, this feeling is not shared by the rest of Scotland; Scottish identity is based on a geography that extends well beyond the western and central lowlands, and on a history in which militant anti-Catholicism and conflicts between Irish Catholic and Protestant working classes play only a small part.

The third main structural feature of Scottish Protestant development concerns the irony of language. A crucial variable in ethnic conflict is a number of dimensions of differentiation that overlap. An important dimension is language and the irony is that Gaelic, which Ulster Catholics can call on as an additional identity device, is, in Scotland, spoken only in the Highlands and Islands, the areas which are the main repositories of conservative Protestantism. Lowland Catholics and Protestants speak the same Scots dialect of English. Lowland Protestants are separated from their Highland co-religionists by the latter speaking a different language.

These features – the possibility of an alternative nationality, encirclement and language differentiation – mark Ulster out from Scotland, and their absence in the Scottish case permits secularization and a degree of cultural assimilation. The lack of these features in the Scottish case allows to take place the changes that I will now elaborate.

The fact that sectarian tension might have been a major part of the concerns of Protestants in the western and central lowlands did not make such tension a major issue for the churches as a whole. The Protestant churches in Scotland were, and are, either genuinely national churches, or, where they were concentrated in one area rather than another, their area of concentration was not the western and central lowlands. Since the reunion of the various branches of Scottish Presbyterianism (completed in 1929) in the Church of Scotland, that body has represented more than 60 per cent of Scottish church members. Like most Western Christian bodies, the Church of Scotland tends to serve principally the middle class, and thus the concerns of the working class in one part of Scotland have not weighed heavy in the minds of the Church's leaders.

Furthermore, the areas where there was, and still is, a strong Orange tradition, are not the main producers of candidates for the ministry. And even if areas such as Bridgeton and Easterhouse produce their quota of ministerial candidates, the training for the ministry – an honours degree course at a university and then three years of theological training – separates the candidate from his background and socializes him into a professional middle-class clergy with national, i.e. Church rather than congregational, interests. Thus even where one has, as in Easterhouse, a population which might provide a congregation with strong Orange sympathies, it is unlikely that it would be pastored by a minister who shared those sympathies. And even if it were, it would only have a small voice in the affairs of the national Church.

Although one would not want to exaggerate their influence, there are also status and economic considerations. Working-class parishes with Orange traditions are often unable to support their own minister and have to be helped out of central funds, that is, carried by wealthier parishes. And the clergy and members have no additional stature deriving from secular dimensions of status. These two points further reduce the influence of anti-Catholicism in the councils of the Church; not only are these parishes relatively few in number and localized, but they each have less than average influence within the organization.

This can be seen in the biographies of the individuals involved in Concern for the Kirk, a conservative alliance formed to combat ecumenism in the Church of Scotland. While a few people involved are both theologically conservative *and* products of an Orange tradition, the others are either one thing or the other. Of the very small number of Church of Scotland ministers who are publicly associated with the Orange Order, one has spent most of his ministry in the Highlands and another in Hawick in the Borders, neither of those places having any Orange tradition.

The main result of the localization of sectarian tension has been to allow the Church of Scotland to change and adapt to modernization in the same way as other major Protestant denominations have done: by becoming liberal in theology and ecumenical in policy. It has been pervaded by a rationalizing impulse in precisely the same way as the Methodists or the English Presbyterians; the special circumstances of Protestant-Catholic hostility in the western and central lowlands have been ignored.

The same features that have permitted the Protestant churches to change away from a theology which could legitimate anti-Catholicism have also allowed changes in the nature and relevance of the Orange Order. It is a matter of debate just quite how religious the Orange Order was at the end of the last century, but it is certain that it was more religious than it is now. The increased secularization was hastened by the fact that the Scottish Orange Order drew its support from a much narrower and lower status base than its counterpart in Ulster. Very few members of the aristocracy or the business and political élites in Scotland have been Orangemen and thus the Order was drawn more heavily on that group – the urban working class – which is least religious. The present leadership consists of people drawn from the respectable upper working class/ lower middle class; a shrinking group which has lost its members either to the new professional middle class or to the proletariat. The class that once supported temperance causes has disappeared. The working class Tory is almost extinct in Scotland. The Liberal Unionists who split with Gladstone over his support for Home Rule in Ireland, and later the Conservatives, were once the natural recipients of the working-class Protestant vote in Scotland but, as the voting patterns since the 1950s show, that support now goes to Labour. This is despite the Labour Party's commitment to a united Ireland and the large proportion of Scottish Labour Party candidates (in Glasgow especially) who are Roman Catholics. One leading Scottish Loyalist said: 'I keep telling the boys to vote for Loyalists and we send round stuff about it and then they go and vote for a Catholic Labour man. Then they're coming up to you and complaining about the Council doing this or that – letting the IRA march in Glasgow.' This Scottish Loyalist votes Conservative because of that party's commitment to the place of Ulster in the United Kingdom, but he has had little success in persuading other Loyalists to do likewise.

Most members and commentators I have interviewed divided the present Orange Order into three groups. The bulk of the members are thought to be working-class people with no active Church commitment; these people did not actively oppose the papal visit. A small leadership cadre remains evangelical, attempts (with little success) to court support from the Church of Scotland, hopes to persuade the Orange social clubs to refrain from opening on Sundays, and strives to build an image of respectability. The third distinct group is made up of the mostly young militants like the Scottish Loyalists, who feel that the leaders have compromised their Protestantism in trying to appear respectable. The leadership has tried to expel the Loyalists but has failed. This third group is more likely than the bulk of the members to vote Conservative rather than Labour but is least likely to have even a nominal Church membership.

The general theme of change in the Orange Order then is fragmentation. The different motives for being Orangemen – preserving the religion, defending the political structure of Britain from Catholic conspiracy, showing solidarity with the Protestants of Ulster, being part of a community – which once coalesced, are now discrete and appeal to different groups of people.

The above observations can be summarized as explanations of why fewer people, a smaller constituency is available for anti-Catholicism. But the same changes also produce a serious crisis of motivation for those people who remain militantly Protestant.

The process of secularization separates politics and religion. It thus divides the two constituencies required for plausible anti-Catholicism. The working-class Protestants who remain antagonistic to Catholics cease to have the religious legitimation for their position, and the middle classes who still have the theology of the conservative Protestantism have no political conflict with Catholics (or place

their desire for stability and respectability above their wish to maintain political Protestantism). This division causes serious problems
for militant Protestant ministers like Jack Glass and David Cassells.
Cassells, like Glass, is an Independent (although he has very close
ties with Ian Paisley's Free Presbyterian Church) with a small congregation in Glasgow and considerable involvement in Protestant activities. He was an Orangeman and chaplain of his lodge. He is the
chairman of the Scottish Constitution Defence Committee, a group
which contains Orangemen and organizes protests against the 'de-
Protestantization' of Scotland's political and educational structures.*

Glass and Cassells are, like most very conservative Protestants,
separatists. They insist on the separation from error and apostasy.
The justification for their own separatist witness requires a constant
concern for doctrinal soundness. Glass goes so far as to practise
double separation; separation not only from error, but also from
those who, though themselves sound, do not actively denounce
error. The concern for soundness threatens alliances with secular
Protestant groups. Glass is forced by the logic of his Calvinism to
denounce the unsaved Orangemen as much as he denounces Roman
Catholicism. He voices frequent scathing criticism of the sham piety
of Orangemen (their drinking on Sundays is especially offensive).
In one sermon he inserted the following aside: 'I wonder how many
Protestants read the Bible. They carry it on the Orange Walk . . .
wrapped in cellophane. It's to keep the rain out . . . keeps the
Orangemen out as well . . . *Real* Protestants are Bible students who
love the Word of God.'

Although Cassells has not yet taken to criticizing 'tribal Protestantism' (his term for what I refer to as 'secular Protestantism') in public,
he too has moved away from active involvement with the Orange
Order, and the poor Orange turnout at the papal visit demonstration
has convinced him of the secular nature of the motivation of most
members.

The problem for militant Protestants like Glass and Cassells is,
then, one of association. The only people who share their militancy
are almost entirely secular groups such as the Apprentice Boys of
Derry and the Scottish Loyalists and they are constrained in working
with such groups by their being as 'unsaved' as the followers of the
Roman Catholicism they wish to condemn. Glass has tried to
develop a rationale which allows him to cope with this difficulty.

---

*David Cassells, an Ulsterman, was educated at the Bible Institute in Glasgow
and pastored the Tent Hall (a mission hall established as a result of the Moody
and Sankey crusade in 1874) until he fell out with the trustees and founded his
own Jock Troup Memorial Church. Although his following is even smaller than
that of Glass, he is the only other representative in Scotland of the militant
Protestant ministry one associates with Ian Paisley.

He argues that religion and politics are separable. In matters political one can work with unsaved Protestants provided the political aims match. It is only in matters religious that one has to oppose all error. Thus he condemns the Orange Order because it claims to be a non-political religious organization. It is thus to be judged on the strict canons of religious orthodoxy, and found wanting. On the other hand, the Apprentice Boys of Derry is a political organization and so there can be co-operation, even to the point of Glass allowing them to hold a service in his church. The irony is that this division of religion and politics is a result of the very secularization which has undermined anti-Catholicism. To accept it, and to claim it as a basis for a strategy that will allow him and other theologically conservative Protestants to resolve the dilemma of militant Protestantism, is to embrace the very principle that has caused the dilemma.

# Chapter 11

# Christianity and New Age Thought

Frank Whaling

*Frank Whaling is a senior lecturer in the divinity faculty at Edinburgh University and a Methodist minister. He delivered this contribution as a lecture in 1991 at a gathering of people interested in both Christianity and New Age ideas. The latter are often assumed to be hostile to the former. Some conservative evangelicals see the New Age as a tool of satan and the upsurge of interest in astrology and alternative therapies as occultist. To others New Agers are simply Greenpeace at prayer, and a symptom of greater interest in the spiritual component of Nature which the established churches are failing to offer. Frank Whaling guides us through the good, the bad and the ugly sides of the New Age, balancing cult and occult against those elements of New Age which are compatible with Christianity.*

During the last few years New Age thought has come into greater prominence. This has happened partly through high-profile, not necessarily representative, practitioners such as David Icke and Shirley MacLaine, and it has happened also through the emergence of New Age insights in more hard-nosed endeavours such as science, industry, economics and education. An example is Stanislav Grof's book *Ancient Wisdom and Modern Science* (1984) in which 'non-religious' scientists express the desire to blend modern science with traditional wisdom. In the last decade there have come to the surface elements connected with what is now known as New Age religion that were mainly hidden before. It is possible to take it too seriously, or not to take it seriously enough. Christians have a lot to learn from New Age thought, they should also be wary of some aspects of it.

It is, of course, true to say that there is no such thing as a New Age world-view. There are many aspects of New Age thought, and indeed a congeries of New Age insights. Marilyn Ferguson's book *The Aquarian Conspiracy*, written in 1980 was taken up by some militant evangelical critics such as Constance Cumbey (in *Hidden Dangers of the Rainbow*, 1983) as signifying a New Age conspiracy to take over the world. This attack was misplaced, both because there was no James Bond-type conspiracy plot built into New Age aims, and because New Age thought and movements are far from being monolithic. In fact, in so far as they can be characterized, New Age adherents tend to be individualistic, relaxed, flexible, free spirits who take somewhat lightly to organization. They are suspicious of dogmas, institutions and establishments. It is not that these do not matter at all, the point is that they are secondary: they are means to ends, not ends in themselves. New Age thought is a network of varied movements and varied ideas that are vaguely linked; it is an amorphous world-view that is nevertheless real.

What then are the elements of New Age thought and religion? For the sake of imposing some sort of framework and clarity, a scheme of ideas will follow, but it is important to remember that the ordered nature of a framework will help to conceal as well as reveal.

An important element in New Age thought is the idea of moving into a new age, of coming to the end of a millennium, of proceeding into the twenty-first century. The build-up to the year 1000 was momentous. The decade leading up to the year 2000 may well prove to be even more awesome, partly because the notion of the end of the millennium is no longer a merely European concern. The year 2000 is etched on to the global calendar, whether it be seen in terms of AD 2000 or 2000 CE (Common Era). This 'new age' is seen not under the heading of Armageddon but as a tremendous invitation to new discoveries, new spiritual adventures and new paradigms. Astrologically the year 2000 coincides with the new Age of Aquarius which promises new freedom and new possibilities.

A second element in New Age thought is the link-up with new paradigms within the philosophy of science. There is a sense that the empiricist and positivistic view of science associated with the names of Descartes and Newton must be extended, widened and deepened. The classical assumptions that we can describe the world fully in scientific language; that scientific language stands in a one-to-one relationship to factual data; that these data are ascertained by observation and experiment; that scientific observation and experiment are based upon what our senses can reveal; that scientific theories are built up through our induction of factual data; that this induction and this theorizing is 'objective' and not reliant upon personal matters; and that scientific knowledge resulting from all this is proven knowledge of the world as it objectively is – these assumptions, from a New Age perspective, form a paradigm that is now being outmoded. They depend upon the primacy of the material, of the senses, and of the classical scientific world-view that has now, it is argued, become limited and is no longer able to deliver the goods. Prominent new theories espoused by much New Age thought include the following: Fritjof Capra's view, in *The Tao of Physics* (1975), that sub-atomic physics is akin to Eastern mysticism in so far as the old view of substance as an objective entity is gone, and the contrast between sub-atomic particles and space around them is overcome; David Bohm's theory of 'implicate order' (*Wholeness and the Implicate Order*, 1988), according to which the universe is enfolded multi-dimensionally upon itself so that, rather like a hologram where any single part of the picture contains the whole, the universe is contained holographically in any particle; Rupert Sheldrake's theory of 'formative causation' (in *A New Science of Life*, 1988); James Lovelock's *Gaia* hypothesis (1982) which suggests that the earth is a living organism, not lifeless matter, and that there is a co-operative mutual dependency between nature and human beings under God; Teilhard de Chardin's older theory of creative evolution (in *The Phenomenon of Man* 1959), incorporating a sense of optimism and hope, which suggests that the cosmic process is evolving in the direction of God; and systems theory in science which concentrates upon the interrelationship of parts within the whole, rather than upon the parts themselves. The latter point is important in New Age thought and religion which imbibes the notion that the point lies not in separate specializations but in holistic thought and synthesis, and in seeing the parts of life and the world in relation to the whole. Thus economics and ecology are intertwined, and if a factory in the Firth of Forth makes a huge profit but spews pollution into the Firth both are relevant to a consideration of its contribution to the general weal. Medicine and alternative medicine are both valuable aids to physical recovery. Moreover, physical and psychological cures are intertwined. Thus New Age thought sees itself as going beyond materialistic and scientistic science in a more metaphysical and spiritual direction. Scientific reductionism is out, and the spiritual world is real. Although some of the scientific theories mentioned above are still speculative, to a number of working scientists there is, if not yet a switch of paradigm, a questioning of aspects of the old paradigm. This can be helpful to Christians who are too often wedded to an old view of science that is now under deep debate.

A third element in New Age thought focuses upon ecology and on female values. In Christian circles this is brought out most clearly in Matthew Fox's creation theology (see, for example, his *The Coming of the Cosmic Christ*, 1988). Both are important in themselves, and both are also global concerns. They are linked too with the recent insight into the complementary nature of the two sides of the brain, the rational and the intuitive. According to this strand of thought there is a need to balance male and female values, a stress upon the outward and a stress upon the inward, an emphasis upon reason and an emphasis upon intuition. Carl Jung's ideas are often leaned upon in this regard, especially his notions of the need to integrate the different sides of the personality, and his notion of the universal unconscious from which all human beings can draw. It is sometimes claimed that New Age thought downplays the whole experience of suffering within humanity, yet Jung does stress the shadow side of the personality which we hide and project on to others. In any event the focus upon ecology and female values is basically sound and the search for a theology that takes ecological and female concerns seriously is one that commends itself to the Christian tradition.

A fourth element in New Age thought relates to healing. In New Age circles there is an abiding sense that the body reflects the total inner state of a human being. Therefore if there is something wrong with the body it is important to heal the body, but it is also important to heal the total personality. Orthodox medicine usually concentrates upon healing the bodily symptom that has manifested the illness. New Age healing would welcome this but would also include the possibility of alternative healing in many different forms, of spiritual healing, and of creative visualization of a well state for the whole person. In this there is an analogy to Christian faith-healing and the possibility of convergence.

A fifth element in New Age thought emphasizes the human potential that is claimed to be the birthright of every person. It is said that human beings undervalue themselves, their possibilities and their potential. As Abraham Maslow puts it (in *Religions, Values and Peak Experiences*, 1987), 'peak experiences' are available to those who are willing creatively to seek them; human beings can and should grow in love; human beings can and should understand themselves as they really are. This is not an option open only to a few. For those who have eyes to see and the vision to seek, the potential lying within human beings is greater than they suppose and it is there for the claiming. This sense that there are no limits to what human beings can do under God is not foreign to the Christian tradition. It was, for example, implied in John Wesley's notion of Christian Perfection which centred upon the idea of growing into perfect love. However, the contrary pull in the direction of human limitation and human unworthiness has also been a factor in Christian self-estimation alongside the injunction to love one's neighbour 'as one loves oneself'. Christian psychiatry has opened up this area of wholesome love of the self, and New Age religion has freely and creatively claimed it as part of true religion.

A sixth element in the New Age complex of ideas emphasizes the power of the inner voice. Meditation of one kind or another is a pervading aspect of New Age religion; spiritual experience is central to the New Age endeavour. God's Spirit is within, and God is immanent. He may be transcendent as well, but above all God is immanent and we can know the Kingdom of God within in our dreams, meditations and leadings. One suspects that a lack of stress upon the Holy Spirit in the Church has led to a deep stress upon the Spirit at two ends of the spectrum – in New Age religion and in charismatic Christianity. Both are interested in healing, both are interested in human potentialities under God, and both are eager to stress the spiritual potential that is available to those who are willing to seek and use it. In both cases there is a challenge to the Church to reawaken to the doctrine and reality of the Holy Spirit. In both cases too there is a challenge to the theory of rampant secularization and the forecast that religion would wither away before the onslaught of science and technology. According to secularization theory, New Age thought and religion and charismatic Christianity should be unlikely and improbable, whereas in fact they are growing and there is a suspicion that a new scientific paradigm is moving in a more spiritual rather than a more secular direction.

Christians can largely affirm the elements that have been mentioned so far: the new science, holistic thought, a concern for ecology, a concern for women's rights, a concern for global issues, and a recognition of the power of healing, human potential and inward spirituality. Vibrant Christians can ally with New Age thought and sometimes are 'new age' in these matters.

Before we consider problems raised for Christianity by New Age thought, it is as well to state that it is different from two constituencies that are sometimes confused with it. New Age religion and thought are different from other living religious traditions. They may borrow from them and often do, especially from Hindu yoga, Buddhist Zen, the Jewish Cabbala, Sufi Islam and American-Indian spirituality. However, New Age thought is not to be equated with other living religions which are often critical of what they see as its radical tendencies. Equally, New Age religion is different from the spectrum of new religious movements, though there may occasionally be some overlap. However, the new religious movements, such as the Unification Church, Hare Krishna, Divine Light Mission, Brahma Kumaris and so on, are usually tightly-knit groups with strong leaders and a strongly worked-out set of ideas, whereas New Age religion tends to be individual, flexible, moving and unstructured. New religious movements may have elements of New Age thought in them, but they are not therefore New Age.

In what respects then should Christians be cautious about New Age thought and religion? Three are worthy of mention. First there is the whole area of channelling whereby a person becomes a medium or a channel for a spirit which delivers teaching or help. The theosophy and anthroposophy movements have arisen during the last century or so based partly upon channelling. However it would be a mistake to label the insights of their leaders as occult obscurantism in spite of the channelling that was part of them. Madame Blavatsky (who together with Colonel Olcott founded the Western theosophical movement), her disciple Annie Besant, and the founder of anthroposophy, Rudolf Steiner, were fascinating people who opened up the inner and spiritual world beyond the physical that humans can relate to through the non-physical dimensions of their being. They and others would claim that they were not declaring anything essentially new but were reclaiming the soul and the spiritual world from the obscuration and captivity that had been their lot since thirteenth-century Christendom. However, one of the ways in which Madame Blavatsky claimed to do this was by spiritual contact with Masters in the Himalayas. Rudolf Steiner claimed to be able to read the 'Akashic Records' which are alleged to be a kind of panorama of spiritual records in the invisible world. Alice Bailey, another mature spiritual thinker who founded the Arcane school in 1923, claimed to receive messages from a Tibetan Master D. K. four thousand miles away. In her case the result was twenty-five books containing impressive insights. However we interpret Madame Blavatsky, Rudolf Steiner and Alice Bailey – were they, for example, tapping into Jung's universal unconscious? – the fact is that in recent years there has arisen a spate of channelling. In 1963 Jane Roberts was writing poetry when a spirit, Seth, came and began to teach through her via trance, and her husband Rob wrote the teaching down. Another well-known spirit, Ramtha, is channelled by another female channeller, J. Z. Knight; and the internationally-known Jack Pursel channels the spirit Lazaris. There are many others. How do we interpret this emergence of channelling? At one level there is evidence of spiritual need and openness, borne out in opinion polls and the work of places such as the Sir Alister Hardy Research Centre at Westminster College, Oxford, to the effect that a large percentage of the population believe in God and have some sort of contact with religious experience, however that is defined. But this is largely outside the orbit of the institutional Christian Church, and is a challenge to the Church to speak to the religious need that is implicitly there. At another level it speaks to an element of gullibility among some New Agers which is probably taken advantage of by some practitioners of channelling for financial gain. However, the example of Jim Bakker and American evangelists who recommend conversion as a way to vast wealth will enable Christians to be humble in these matters. At yet another level there is the need for caution: channelling spirits has some similarities to the helping role of the Virgin Mary and the saints in the Roman Catholic and Orthodox communities, but it is also different. It is not so much that channelling can have a dark side, as some evangelicals claim, as that it becomes so banal, and is a diversion (in New Age as in Christianity) from direct contact with God.

A second question that may be applied to New Age thought relates to its interpretation of psychic and spiritual power. These may overlap, but they may also be different. New Age spirituality tends to hold them together, but an ability to 'discern the spirits' has usually been valued by authentic religion of any kind. Psychic power is not good or bad in itself; it is neutral. It contains no necessary ethical content. The odic force that can be used in healing for example, is a psychic human gift that can be used both within and outside of a religious milieu. It is helpful when used in the light of ethical and spiritual perception. 'By their fruits ye shall know them' remains a valid criterion not only for the exercise of spiritual power but also for the exercise of psychic power.

A third cautionary note relates to challenges made by some New Age thought to Christian doctrines, for example the doctrine of Christ. Especially interesting and controversial are the references that are sometimes made to the lost years of Jesus. Did he stay as a carpenter in Nazareth? Speculations such as those of the Rosicrucians are one thing; historical certainty about events in the life of Jesus that are necessarily speculative are another. When Shirley MacLaine states in *Going Within* (1989) that 'of course Jesus was an Essene teacher and healer' there is no 'of course' about it, as any knowledgeable scholar will readily testify. She appears to have received this insight from Edmond Szekely's *The Discovery of the Essene Gospel of Peace* (1975) and treated it as fact. Other books that are more certain than they have any right to be about the hidden years of the life of Jesus are Notovitch's *La Vie inconnue de Jésus Christ* written in 1894, and Levi Downing's *The Aquarian Gospel of Jesus the Christ* written in 1907. Included in Notovitch's book is a document entitled 'The Life of Saint Issa: Best of the Sons of Men' which he claims to have discovered in Ladakh and which he claims is superior to the evidence in the canonical Gospels. Some of the accounts of the hidden years of Jesus claim that the three magi visited the two-year-old Jesus and began to initiate him as a Master; that at the age of thirteen he went to Persia and to India, was trained in Hinduism and Buddhism, and was initiated as a Master; that after the events in Palestine that led to his crucifixion he did not die on the cross but (and sometimes evidence from the Turin shroud is introduced) he survived and went off again to India, and was finally buried in Kashmir. Clearly this is speculative history and speculative theology. Helen Schucman's claim to have transcribed her influential 1,200-page *Course in Miracles* (1985) through the voice of Jesus, and the estimable counsellor Edgar Cayce's claim to tap into the Akashic Records about Jesus with his unconscious mind, do not diminish the sense that speculation is at work. So often New Age speculation about Jesus is presented as fact, and at that point it is fair for Christians to ask searching questions. It is wise to repeat what was stated at the beginning, that New Age thought is diverse and operates at different levels and it is a minority of New Agers who would adopt stridently anti-Christian views. Naivete rather than malevolence is more often at work.

It is helpful to differentiate between two kinds of New Age thought: the soft-core version outlined in the first half of this Chapter which could be taken up and affirmed by Christians, and the hard-core version outlined later which should be treated with caution. There is evidence of a bridge that is being built between New Age thought and Christianity whereby some Christians are widening and deepening their Christian faith through contact with New Age thought, and whereby some people are finding that New Age thought is a way into Christianity, albeit at a deeper level than was the case before (if, in fact, they were Christians before).

New Age thought is a phenomenon that is most present in the West. It is in the West that a sense of 'soul' and a sense of the 'spiritual world' have most obviously disappeared. New Age thought is a challenge and a spur to the Christian tradition in the West to rediscover the importance of living, inward, spirituality that takes Spirit seriously and does not bow down to secular models as the norm. When New Agers ask where they can find a local church that takes spirituality seriously, where are they to be directed? It is a challenge and a spur also to think creatively and adventurously about some wider secular issues of the day: the way forward for modern science, ecology, women's rights, global issues, healing, human potential, hope for the world, the need for a new world order, the desirability of taking into account all parts of the person-ality – body, mind and spirit – and the desirability of taking into account all dimensions of life – the material, the mental and the spiritual.

It is true to say that inward spirituality has never been lost in the Christian tradition. It has been maintained especially within the monastic communities of the Orthodox, Roman Catholic and Angli-can churches. However, its influence and importance have declined in face of the material and outward success of science and technology and secular models. The spur to the revival of Christian spirituality has come from outside and has led to a rediscovery and renewal of what was already implicitly present within the Christian tradition. It was triggered by Hindu swamis and Zen masters in the 1960s, especially in America but also in Britain, and it has been reinvigor-ated by New Age figures such as Sir George Trevelyan who have linked a revival of spirituality with the holistic and adventurous world-view mentioned earlier. As Trevelyan puts it:

> The spiritual world-view . . . sees the world of Creative Spirit as primary – a realm of Absolute Being and Creative Intelligence, from which matter and the phenomenal or material world are derived. Understanding, in the spiritual world-view, involves the capacity to look inward and so through into spheres of ever-widening consciousness . . . The spiritual world-view is a vision of wholeness, an apprehension of the essential unity of all life . . . The emerging world-view is essentially simple. Grasping it requires

no great intellectual effort, only a flexibility of thought, a readiness to delight in change, a resilience and youthfulness of attitude, regardless of how many years we have lived. (*A Vision of the Aquarian Age: the Emerging Spiritual World-View*, 1984, pp. 6–7,6)

It is perhaps no accident that New Age thought and religion are strong where contemporary Western Christianity is somewhat weak, and it may also be the case that the opposite is true and that New Age thought and religion are somewhat weak where contemporary Western Christianity is strong. Having said that, it may well be the case that the seeming 'weaknesses' of New Age thought and religion – a lack of firm structures, a lack of clear doctrines and a flexible tolerance – also constitute New Age strength. Like 'Star Trek' it is willing to go where humans – and angels – often fear to venture in its daring quest for a deep spirituality and a planetary and humane vision that will, naively or otherwise, match up to the stimulus of the new century, the new millennium. Rather than sit on the sidelines or negatively criticize, it behoves Christians to do likewise on the model of the early Fathers who felt the call, in humility rather than arrogance, spiritually to outlive and mentally to outthink the world of their time.

# Chapter 12

# *In Memoriam*: George MacLeod

Ronald Ferguson

*Ron Ferguson is minister of St. Magnus Cathedral in Orkney, but began life as a journalist. This training stood him in excellent stead as Community Minister in Easterhouse where he started a community newspaper, and in writing the highly acclaimed biography of George MacLeod, founder of the Iona Community. Ron Ferguson was leader of the Community on its fiftieth anniversary when he had the pleasant task of welcoming Lord MacLeod back to Iona at the age of ninety-three to dedicate the centre named after him. When Macleod died in 1991, it was natural that Ron Ferguson should give the oration at a memorial service in Govan Old parish church and it is the text of that sermon which is reproduced as his contribution to this volume.*

I have two texts. The first is from the Second Epistle to Timothy, chapter 4, verse 7: 'I have fought the good fight: I have finished the race: I have kept the faith.'

The second is from a piece of writing by George MacLeod. It's not from one of his great sermons or broadcasts, but a throwaway remark in a letter to Douglas Alexander: 'I don't know why I went to Iona. God wanted it, and it was such a hell of a gamble that He could only find George MacLeod, who lost £40 one night at poker when he was waiting to be demobbed from the Agile and Suffering Highlanders.'

I remember it well. I was in the refectory of Iona Abbey, when I was approached by a young and earnest member of staff, who was something of a classics scholar. He had been reading the Rule of the Iona Community – the little book which describes what it is that members of the Community commit themselves to when they join. He was troubled by the fact that the book was titled *Miles Christi*, which means 'Soldier of Christ'.

'How could George MacLeod, who is a pacifist, use such a military title?' he asked me. 'And why is it *miles*, singular, instead of *milites*, plural, when he is talking about a community?'

At that moment, as if on cue, the refectory door opened and in came the old thespian himself.

'There's George MacLeod – why don't you ask him?' I told the young man. And he did.

George thought for a moment, then he replied: 'I called it *Soldier of Christ* because we are engaged in a battle . . . And I called it "Soldier", singular, instead of "Soldiers", plural, because when I made up the Rule I was the only Christian in the Community at the time!'

Exit ninety-year-old actor-manager on left, chuckling.

George MacLeod was what my aunty from Cowdenbeath would have called 'an awfy man'. And 'awfy' could be awfy awfy. He could be stubborn, imperious, insensitive, ruthless and manipulative. But George was 'awfy' in the other sense too – aweful and inspiring. Most people in this church today would have leapt out of the trenches with and for George – and that's why we're here today. Not to put it too sentimentally, I loved him like I loved my own father.

What can one say about George MacLeod that hasn't been said already? I've written more than 400 pages and used up many rain forests to try to capture the man – and still there's something elusive about him, thank God. We know all the clichés – a spiritual giant, one of the greatest Scotsmen of this century etc. Let's not bore George silly by repeating them.

The first occasion on which I encountered the man was when I was a young reporter with the *Edinburgh Evening News*. I was covering the General Assembly. When George started to speak, the words came pouring out in torrents, and I couldn't take him down in shorthand. Nor could the other reporters. We put our pencils down and listened, spellbound. He was that kind of orator.

The second time I met him was on Iona, when I went there as a student for the ministry. It so happened it was Community Week, when all the members of the Iona Community gather on the island. On the Wednesday pilgrimage, at the Marble Quarry, I listened, spellbound again, as George went through the history of the world in about three minutes. Huge, sweeping, soaring generalizations. Whatever George MacLeod lacked, it wasn't confidence. In the middle of this oratorical *tour de force*, I heard a Community member behind me, say in a stage whisper: 'How does he get away with it?' At that moment, in that stage whisper, I understood something of the relationship between George MacLeod and the Iona Community. How does he get away with it?

Let's not canonize George MacLeod, or imprison him in stained glass. Some people think that to meet this spiritual giant must have been the most ethereal and mystical of experiences. It was nothing of the kind. It was more like being *mugged*. You were safer on the streets of inner-city Glasgow at three o'clock in the morning than outside Iona Abbey in broad daylight when George MacLeod was on the rampage. What was even more lethal was to accept his invitation to whisky. That was to invite total brain melt-down, a taking leave of your senses, a consideration of possibilities which should never be seriously entertained in sobriety.

Most of us in this church have been spiritually mugged by George MacLeod, and we bear the marks in our life. And we're glad of it. That's why we're here. Because we have been wounded and lamed, and we wouldn't have it otherwise.

What can we say about him? He was a true soldier – a fighting man of immense bravery. You know, all his life he preferred the company of military men to pacifists. All his life he was a soldier looking for his lost regiment. All his life he was looking for battles to fight. He truly fought the good fight.

But above all else he was a *gambler*. And how the Church desperately needs gamblers today. He played cards for money in the trenches. He gambled his life in the Second Battle of Ypres, and came out alive but scarred. And when God needed a gambler for Iona, MacLeod was his man.

It's awesome today to stand in this pulpit where George MacLeod stood in May 1938 to bid farewell to the congregation he loved. When we see the restored abbey on Iona today, it all seems so right. We forget that in May 1938, with the storm clouds of war gathering over Europe, George MacLeod was taking an enormous gamble. He was leaving the security of the parish ministry, and of an assured career structure. When he was scratched, the man bled Moderator. It was in his blood. Yet he embarked on a wild goose scheme on a remote island, without ecclesiastical backing and without the necessary money.

'Could I have said No?' he told the Govan congregation. 'Could I have said: "I am safe and happy in Govan and I am not going to take any risks whether half of Scotland goes pagan or not"? Or again, could I have gone on getting into the Govan pulpit and saying to our young people, "Christianity is an adventure; you must have faith; you must be prepared to take risks for Christ" and things like that (which I so often say), if in my heart I had known – and you had not known – that all these pointers had once come to me and I had skirted round them and had stayed on in a much safer billet than the one I am going to?'

Could he have said No? Well, yes, actually, he could have. He could have said no. But he didn't. And what an achievement that rebuilding was! And at what cost. To others. Just like *The Spire*, in William Golding's novel. What ruthless, frightening dedication it required! And the rebuilding was achieved at a cost to George himself. Despite his apparent confidence, every time he stood at Fionnphort and looked over to Iona, he had a knot in his stomach just like he had when he went out to the Front in the First World War. I find that reassuring.

One way to understand the life of George MacLeod is to set it to music and see it as a Western in your own mind: with George in the role of the gambler. You always knew when George MacLeod was in town. The saloon doors burst open. George liked nothing better than a High Noon – he enjoyed a good fight the way some people enjoy bad health. He was no meek and mild pacifist – he was a *gunslinging* pacifist. What he never fully understood, when he strode boldly down the street, was the number of sniper rifles trained on him from dilapidated buildings. Or maybe he did.

George MacLeod was a *hero*, a frontiersman, a mythic figure. Like Columba. This is supposed to be the age of the anti-hero, and heroes are very unfashionable today. But we need them at a very deep level. In one of the great books of this century, *The Denial of Death*, Ernest Becker says that the urge to cosmic heroism is sacred and mysterious: and that we need 'new heroisms that are basically matters of belief and will, of dedication to a vision'. George MacLeod was a hero in that towering sense. That is quite different from being a *celebrity* – those hyped-up creatures of the media who are legends only in their own lunchtime.

He was also a perfect model of what Søren Kierkegaard called the 'Knight of Faith' – a member of an aristocracy of creative risk-takers for God. And it is impossible to give the gifts of the knight of faith without first being dubbed a knight by a Higher Majesty. That is the true aristocratic club to which George belonged, and the only one worth bothering about. It was the aristocracy of the pure in heart, those who single-mindedly serve God's purposes.

In America five years ago, George was asked by a minister how it was that he had managed to stay so single-minded all his life. When I relayed the question into George's ear, he replied: 'I have remained so single-minded all these years by being deaf!'

But there's more to it than that. In spite of his sophistication, George had a child-like faith. I am reminded of Karl Barth, author of *Church Dogmatics*. When asked by the media what the heart of his message was, the great Professor thought for a minute then sang softly:

> Jesus loves me this I know
> For the Bible tells me so.

That childlike faith of George's was matched by a deep intuition, which allowed him to know things he couldn't fully explain. He didn't really understand science. He would quote Einstein repeatedly but he never read any of Einstein, never mind wrestled with his thinking. How *did* he get away with it? And yet he *understood*. How maddening!

Who can forget:

> Invisible we see you, Christ beneath us.
> With earthly eyes we see beneath us stones and dust and dross,
> fit subjects for the analyst's table.
> But with the eye of faith, we know you uphold.
> In you all things consist and hang together;
> The very atom is light energy,
> the grass is vibrant
> the rocks pulsate.
>
> All is in flux; turn but a stone and an angel moves.

He had the lyrical heart of a Celtic poet. In his prayers and in his theology and in his life we have the fusion of the spiritual and the material – perhaps his greatest and most majestic gift to us.

Some people will feel that in a service centring on George MacLeod we should only be talking about ideas, and not the man himself, because that's what he surely would have done. I want to resist that notion. Because it is precisely in the flesh-and-blood man, in all his human frailties, that we have seen something of the glory of God. That is how God works. Truth is mediated through personality, incarnated, rooted, messy. All theology is, at the end of the day, biography. Even when it's the biography of God. And, like you, I want to celebrate that life – particularly its heroism, its risk-taking, its flair, its passion, its romance, its excitement. It is a flawed life – the theological and psychological fault-lines are there for all to see – but what a life!

And what of the future? It surely does not belong in imitating George MacLeod. God save us all from mini-MacLeods, or from George MacLeod fundamentalists! One of the reasons for writing George's biography was to make it impossible to be a Macleod fundamentalist. George said so many different and contradictory things at different times that anyone trying to found a New Church of True Believers in George MacLeod deserves not just a dull life but a demented one as well.

What should we recommit our lives to, in gratitude for the life of George MacLeod? Can we work for a Church of Scotland which follows the Govan Gambler in taking risks, in going for broke? Can Scotland know that there truly is a Church in town? If we are going to go down the tubes, let us at least do it with style! The Kirk today is not short of decency and worthiness. But imagination and flair are not part of our strong suit.

Let us have a moratorium on 'Urgent Calls to the Kirk' and 'Urgent Calls to the Nation' and let us instead celebrate the gospel with laughter and tears and passion and style. Let us stop lecturing and hectoring the nation, and let's instead throw a party on the Mound and invite all of Scotland to join us.

You see, people cannot live by bread alone. They need a spiritual vision. But it will not come from an upright, moralizing, tight-arsed Kirk, but one which is truly liberated. We are too sober by half, too prudent for our own good and the world's good. Let's get out of the kailyard and the morass of *Sunday Post* moralizing, and spend all that we've got. Let's abandon what Iain Crichton Smith calls 'Survival without error' and go for double or quits. Let's lose our life in a gamble which may mean that we will truly find it. Or maybe not.

And while we're at it, let's have a truly ecumenical Church.

George MacLeod, who through the sign of the rebuilt Iona Abbey has taught so many of us what it means to be ecumenical, is right again: the only ecumenical movement that is worth anything is one in which we are so close to one another that we can be *rude* to one another. Like George MacLeod, I want to be rude to my Roman Catholic brothers and sisters about the issue of inter-communion. I want to say to you in all honesty: 'Despite all your theological sophistication, I don't think you fully realize what you are doing to us all.' If I hear any more hand-wringing talk about the unavoidable pain of our unhappy divisions, I think I will scream. In fact, I want to scream that pain. In a day when there are so many exciting alternative religious options for people, our historic Christian divisions feel more and more like archaic and self-indulgent obstacles.

Here's something that we Christians should give up for Lent and beyond: all talk of Christianity as a religion of reconciliation. As we sit back to back at separate tables, we are a laughing stock, and not all the sophisticated talk in the world about the non-negotiable nature of truth can cover our nakedness. Any little kid in Govan can see that at this stage the Christian emperor has no clothes.

Having been involved in a number of ecumenical ventures, I believe that George MacLeod is right: as well as polite ecumenical conversations, we need the liturgical and street theatre of outright shame. And I hope that our Roman Catholic sisters and brothers will feel free to be rude to those of us who are Protestant, about *our* failings: for instance, about the lack of mystery and poetry of our worship, where so much of our liturgy has all the grace and beauty of a Strathclyde Regional memo or a DSS pamphlet about heating allowances for pensioners.

Yes, we need an ecumenical movement which faces the issues and takes risks. Iona Abbey, which is home for all denominations, is a place for such risk-taking.

Wouldn't it be marvellous if, in the year 2000, the Pope came to Iona Abbey and marked two millennia of Christianity by inaugurating a new era of Christian freedom and adventure: celebrated by offering the bread and wine to all believers! People would then know that there was a real church in town: an emperor with some clothes – even if they're from the Oxfam shop. And perhaps even nailprints in his hands.

And who knows, perhaps Christianity itself will undergo a transformation equivalent to the overcoming of the split between Jew and Gentile. The words of George MacLeod's grandfather, the great Norman, are pertinent here: 'Where is the germ of the church of the future? . . . Neither Calvinism, nor Presbyterianism, nor Thirty-Nine Articles, nor High Churchism nor Low Churchism, nor any existing organization can be the church of the future! May God give us patience to wait!'

We need to be inspired by George MacLeod, but also to transcend his limitations. Can we commit ourselves to work for a Church and society in which the qualities of the feminine are honoured as much as those of the masculine, the intuitive as much as the rational? If our religious and political institutions are to be transformed, we need to start right here. We live in very exciting times. It is an exciting time to be the Church. Did you think you would live to see the day when the Berlin Wall would come down? When Nelson Mandela would be released from prison? When the Communist Party would be legal in Britain and banned in Russia?

Can we have a Church which rejoices at the overthrow of tyrannical communism in Russia and Eastern Europe and at the same time asks tough questions about how democratic and accountable our own institutions are? Peace and disarmament and justice are now on the world's agenda in a way which George MacLeod could only have dreamed of – and did dream of – a few years ago. And the challenge to all of us now is to move from slogans to specifics, from knee-jerk responses to creative solutions.

Can we have a Church in Scotland – and of course beyond Scotland – which will work passionately and imaginatively for peace and disarmament, and for justice for the world's poor and hungry? A Church which forces these matters on to the political agenda, and ensures that elections aren't simply about our own precious standard of living?

When George MacLeod was awarded the Templeton International Prize in 1989, he wasn't interested in the glory. He wanted the *money*. And he wanted it to give it all away to the causes most dear to his heart: peace and the ending of poverty.

One thing George would never forgive me for in this service would be if I were to allow more than 1,000 people to leave this church without being asked to sign up for a new crusade. So as you leave there will be a petition. We can do no less for George.

It simply calls on all the political parties of this country to ensure that the issues of peace and justice for the world's poor are made central to the debate at the next general election. Perhaps at the next election, as well as the West Lothian Question, we can have the

George MacLeod Question: How can the 'peace dividend' which comes from the ending of the Cold War be invested in the future of the poor of the world?

I began with the old actor-manager in the refectory of Iona Abbey. I close with the same man in the new reconciliation centre of Iona which bears his name. When we first took George into the New MacLeod Centre, a few days before the official opening in 1988, the first thing he did was to repeat the Lord's Prayer in a loud voice. We were touched by this display of piety. Then the old rogue turned, and said with a twinkle: 'I was only testing the accoustics!'

After the opening ceremony, George and Leah Tutu and some of us linked arms and almost danced into the Centre. George, without his sticks, was almost airborne. And as we all sang the South African spiritual 'We are marching in the light of God', George's voice sounded uncannily like that of a child. 'Marching in the Light of God' is what George's life has been about. Let us march in his company, inspired by him without being commanded by him. Let us dance along with him, and sing the Resurrection songs with child-like voices.

Let us fight the good fight. Let us finish the race. Let us keep the faith; remembering that

> those who wait on the Lord shall renew their strength:
> they shall mount up on wings as eagles:
> they shall run and not be weary:
> they shall walk and not faint.

Or to put it in the words of the hymn which will shortly be sung for the first time:

> Think not to to weary
> or lay your great commission down;
> nor crave approval
> nor fear the critic's frown.
> prevail through tears, love with laughter,
> risk all, then hereafter
> receive from Christ your crown.

George MacLeod, *Miles Christi*, Soldier of Christ: you have fought the good fight. You have finished the race. You have kept the faith.

George MacLeod, Gambler of Govan: when will we see your likes again?

*Chapter 13*

# The Atonement

## D. W. D. Shaw

*D. W. D. (Bill) Shaw began his working life as a lawyer. He became a theologian after an assistantship with Murdo Ewen Macdonald in St. George's, Edinburgh, then (c. 1960) a fashionable church at which queues were to be seen on Sunday evenings. The two men, the fiery preacher and the urbane lawyer, were a formidable team and together climbed the Munroes mountains (all Scottish, over 3000ft). Bill Shaw won distinction as a squash international. In his other sport, golf, he is chaplain to the R & A at St. Andrews and holds the honour of having been principal of two divinity colleges (New College, Edinburgh and St. Mary's, St. Andrews). In the theological spectrum, he could be classified under 'process theology', and this is reflected in his contribution, delivered as a sermon for a BBC Scotland radio broadcast.*

Your world was a world without hope and without God. But now in union with Christ Jesus, you who once were far off have been brought near by the shedding of Christ's blood. For he is himself our peace. Gentiles and Jews, he has made the two one, and in his own body of flesh and blood has broken down the enmity which stood like a dividing wall between them; for he annulled the law with its rules and regulations, so as to create out of the two a single new humanity in himself, thereby making peace. (Eph. 2:13–15)

I have chosen this rather difficult text because I want to do something rather unfashionable. I want to try to preach a doctrinal sermon, and the Christian doctrine I want to speak about is known as the doctrine of Atonement. That is the belief which Christians hold that the life, death and resurrection of Jesus, particularly his passion and death, have made a unique difference to the life of our world, past, present and future. The belief is that this has made a difference, a difference affecting nothing less than the relation between ourselves and our world to God. The doctrine of atonement is the Church's attempt to give expression to this difference.

The first thing I want to say is that it is only an *attempt*. There is no one correct way of understanding what God has done for us in

Christ. The Bible itself does not provide this. What it does is to refer to it in a dozen different ways or pictures in words or images which have the best chance of being understood by the people to whom they were addressed. There was no alternative to this and there is no alternative to this. The reason is that, fortunately or unfortunately (I think, for reasons which will become apparent later, fortunately), there is no holy language in which this could be expressed, no language immune from change or misunderstanding. All we have is our ordinary language, all we can do is to try as best and as faithfully as we can to remain true to the intention and witness of the first disciples and their experience as we have it in scripture, and to the experience of the Christian community in the past, the Church: but we also have to try to be true to our own experience and our own ways of thinking and talking, which are not necessarily those of the past. Now this may sound disappointing, vague and precarious. But there is no alternative to it – not as long as we have no holy language to fall back on. So with this in mind, how are we to try to express and understand the atonement in our time, in our language? For the language of a bygone age will not necessarily do.

At one time, for example, when the world seemed to be full of spirits and demons they were responsible for everything, good or bad, that happened. If you sneezed, even, or had a cold, you would put it down to possession by some spirit; at that time it made sense, it meant something desperately important to speak of Christ's work being a victory over all the evil spirits that plagued and distorted life. But, we don't live in that kind of world – or most of us don't – and so that kind of language doesn't make much sense to us any more. Neither does the language the medieval world used when they spoke of Christ's death in terms of 'satisfaction', a legal term, familiar enough in feudal times but quite alien to us now. So how are we to express it?

Fortunately, the Bible itself has many different ways of expressing what was achieved by Christ's life, and especially by his death, and one way – the way of our text – is to think of it as *the breaking down of a wall*. Good fences may make good neighbours, they say (though I doubt it), but the effect of a wall, whatever its builders' intention, is to block communication. You didn't need to live in Berlin – East or West – to realize the offensiveness or the menace of a wall. Nor do you have to see with your own eyes, as many of us do quite frequently, the sombre outside of Saughton Prison or Barlinnie, to say nothing of the inside. The writer of the letter to the Ephesians in the passage that was read was speaking of the hitherto indestructible dividing wall that existed between Jews and Gentiles, that wall which he claimed had been broken down, broken through once and for all by God's action in Christ. But there are plenty of other walls which we could recognize if we would in our world, in our lives.

Walls which in so many different situations prevent communication: between husband and wife; between management and labour; between parents and children; between East and West, or perhaps even more serious now between the rich North and the poor South. These walls and many others – I appeal to your imagination to recognize them – are surely real enough, and we don't seem to be making too good a job at getting rid of them. But in Christian perspective, there is one wall that encloses all the other walls, and that is the one which separates the unsatisfactory, touchy, supersensitive self that I am from the self that I might even have it in me to be, that wall, in a word, which separates me from God.

This wall – and this is the gospel – has been broken through once and for all from the side of God, by what has happened in Christ. But if that is not to be just pious rhetoric, what does that mean? I think the clue here, or at least one clue, may be the notion of 'identification'. You know what it means to identify with someone. You don't cease to be yourself but you try to put yourself in someone else's shoes. You try to see the world as they see it, and feel what they are feeling. Now the only people we can go any distance in identifying with are those we really care for: our children, for example, or people we really love. For the rest, we can try to identify, but unless we happen to be someone like Mother Teresa in Calcutta, we lack the knowledge, the concern, the imagination really to know what it would be like to be in someone else's shoes. The point I'm trying to make is this: we know what it means to identify with someone else; the more we care, the better we are able to identify; but only a perfect love can identify completely. Now that is exactly the claim of the gospel. Such is the love of God that, in Jesus of Nazareth, he has identified with us, with stupid, selfish, ignorant human beings – 'sinful humanity' would be the traditional way of putting it. Identified with us by coming the whole way – with no reservations, no holds barred – in a solidarity that refuses to be broken, even by death. This is why with the death of Jesus, the New Testament sees not the anger of God or the cruelty of God but the love of God reaching its deepest, widest, most intense point. Even divine love can go no further than this. But in going this total length of identification, God has unambiguously achieved the breakthrough of the final wall of separation, has declared that he is after all on our side, that he accepts us, forgives us, and offers us a share in his love.

The wall broken through – but not without cost. A not unreasonable question that is sometimes asked is this: why all this stress on the suffering and death of Christ? If God really does love us, why can he not just forgive, just like that? There are many possible ways of answering this, but the answer that appeals to me is the one given forty years ago now by a great Scottish theologian, D. M.

Baillie. He appealed to our ordinary human experience. If I wrong a friend, he suggested, if I let him down in some way, if my friend really cares for me, for him to forgive me will be no easy casual matter. Not because the friend's feelings are hurt or even because he feels let down. Rather the more he cares for me, the more he will feel the shame I should feel for letting him down. Do you see the point? If God really loves us, will he not somehow have to suffer the pain of our wrongdoing, our guilt before he can forgive us? This is exactly what Christians see happening in the passion and death of Jesus, and I venture to suggest that they could see it all the more clearly if they could stick to this notion of God identifying with them in Christ. No breakthrough, then, without suffering.

This way of atonement, this way of reconciliation through identification also means: *no breakthrough without risk*. For if God's identification with us is complete, then this must mean that love comes on our terms, not his, that it comes not parading its credentials but in truly human form, with no bullet-proof vest and no hot line of rescue. It must take the risk of not being recognized, or misunderstood or turned away. Is this too great a risk? I can only ask you, which is the greater love: one which comes in protective clothing, guaranteed against rejection? Or one which takes the risk of coming the whole way for the sake of the loved ones, with all that that implies? Surely the latter, for only the latter can beget a response in freedom and love, only the latter is God's. No breakthrough, then, without risk.

But – most important of all – *no breakthrough, without consequences*. What is the effect of the breakthrough? We could say in a word that communication is restored. Not automatically, of course, and not without personal involvement. But the connection is made, the basis is restored, the exchange is working and the lines are open. Because of what God has done in Christ, we really have been given new opportunities which were not open to us to opt for before. I mean that we don't have to do the things we've always done, we don't have to hold to the attitudes we've always had, we don't have to travel the same route that's become our routine. Because of God's forgiveness, we don't need to prove ourselves to God or anyone else, or pretend, to anyone else or to ourselves, to be other than we are. Because of his acceptance, we can accept ourselves, and yet, however old, however set in our ways, talk in terms of new beginnings. Surely, we can't put back the clock. But we can look forward, and taking a step towards our neighbour, take a step through the gap in that wall. That same love which has blasted through invites us to respond, to share and finally to dare to tread the same path of identification with those who in our world are afar.

*Chapter 14*

# Not Quite the Last Word

Murdo Ewen Macdonald

*Murdo Ewen Macdonald was born in Harris and was ordained on the eve of the Second World War. He eschewed chaplaincy and fought as a combatant in the paratroops but was captured and spent much of the war in Stalag Luft III, scene of the Great Escape. He is still much in demand as a speaker at gatherings of his fellow POWs in the USA and is married to an American. This pulpit giant of the post-war generation became professor of practical theology at Trinity College, Glasgow University, and is the author of several books of sermons. His contribution was written as an epilogue for a forthcoming autobiography. It reflects his socialist beliefs as well as the eloquence of someone who has mastered English as a second language after Gaelic.*

It was George Bernard Shaw, with characteristic percipience, who remarked: 'You know what a person believes not from the creed he formally professes, but from the assumptions on which he habitually acts.'

Throughout my life I have had many concerns, but only a few dominant ones. These are passionate interests that gathered up my scattered unco-ordinated energies and have given them a sense of purposeful direction.

One of these dominant concerns is politics. In the Hebridean community in which I was brought up, ordinary uneducated crofters were deeply interested in politics. At their Ceilidhs they could knowledgeably discuss the virtues and vices of the Prime Minister, the Chancellor of the Exchequer and the Home Secretary.

Among Christians there is a deep-seated aversion to mixing religion and politics. One reason is historical. In the past the Church's involvement in politics was far from edifying. The historian Professor Herbert Butterfield, himself a devout Christian, claims that when the Church occupied the seat of power, it was every bit as ruthless as communism. In the present the savagery of the Provisional IRA, and of the extremist elements of right-wing Protestants in Northern Ireland, illustrates what I mean.

Another reason is the tacit assumption among many Christians that the proper sphere of religion is spiritual, while the proper sphere of politics is physical, the material needs of men and women; in sum the world here and now.

The divorce between the spiritual and the secular has its roots deep in antiquity. It goes back to the Manichaean heresy with which the great Augustine for a time flirted. It was the belief that the spirit was good and that the body was bad. Persian in origin, in due course it penetrated Christianity. It became so powerful and pervasive that some of the early Church Fathers were openly hostile to sex. Origen got himself castrated.

The Old Testament prophets did not recognize any spiritual dichotomy. To them religion was an intensely personal business. Jehovah called each one of them by name. It was he who summoned them to leave the vines they were dressing and the herds they were tending, to witness in the maelstrom of Middle East politics.

The privatization of religion never once occurred to them. The God they proclaimed was Sovereign Lord of all History. The distinction so many Christians insist on drawing between individual and social salvation they would find utterly incomprehensible.

The Manichaean heresy, the exaltation of man's spirit and the denegration of his body is still with us. It sits in every pew in every church in the land. Right-wing and left-wing governments are about equally hostile to clerics meddling in politics. This was true of Stalin and Hitler. It is also true of Mrs Margaret Thatcher.

By the time I was halfway through my first degree at university, I knew I was a socialist of some kind or other. Let me make it plain that I have never had any truck with the frenetic hard-line extremists on the right and on the left who are incapable of changing their minds however much the human situation changes. Victims of an arrested development, they have no place in politics.

Most preachers are careful never to get mixed up in politics. They take refuge in sonorous generalities and innocuous banalities. Worshippers in the pew haven't a clue which side they support. On the other hand a minister must not use the pulpit as a party political platform. The preacher who does this is guilty of grossly abusing his high office. Congregations have every right to resent it.

Nevertheless, a minister can with a good conscience pronounce on issues which transcend party politics. Issues like health, education, apartheid and the nuclear dimension. The preacher must do this intelligently and sensitively. There must be no attempt to gain any partisan ideological advantage.

On television, radio and public platforms I have condemned the piling up of nuclear weapons, the insanity of the overkill. I am not a conventional pacifist but I am an atomic pacifist. Immensely indebted to Arthur Koestler, in sermons and lectures I have argued

that we are living within the New Calendar. The Old Calendar came
to an end on 6 August 1945. Let me explain. Before that day mankind
lived with the prospect of death as individuals. In the obscene
carnages of the battles of the Somme, Passchendaele and Stalingrad,
each soldier died as an individual. But the moment the first atomic
bomb outshone the sun when it burst over Hiroshima, in a thou-
sandth fraction of a second we moved from the Old Calendar to the
New Calendar. That means that mankind now lives with the prospect of death not as individuals but as a species.

Pro-nuclear advocates maintain that the balance of terror is the
sole guarantee of peace. A curious argument! I agree with Bertrand
Russell. If there is going to be a nuclear war it will probably come
about as a result of accident not design. At a circus we can reasonably expect an acrobat to be able to walk the tight-rope for five
minutes, ten, perhaps twenty, but he can't go on doing it indefinitely. The nuclear powers can't possibly go on playing a game of
Russian roulette *ad infinitum*.

Another dominant concern is education. Above all others this is
the one which provoked criticism, sometimes amounting to vicious
hostility. At university and later on in the army, I became more and
more suspicious of an expensive élitist form of education. Of course
the private sector produces highly articulate, brilliant students. It
would be surprising if it didn't. It also produces nincompoops who,
because they speak with correct upper-class accents, occupy positions for which they are lamentably ill-equipped. An influential
section of the British public tend to equate intonation with education.

Right-wing Victorians held that heredity was the sole determinant
of intelligence. Marxists supported the opposite view. They claimed
that all normal children were potentially equal in intelligence.
According to them environment not heredity was the only determinant.

My guess is that right-wing Victorians and left-wing Marxists
were guilty of special pleading. I also suspect that the élitists have
persistently overestimated the influence of heredity and played
down the importance of environment. They have proceeded on the
assumption that the educational race goes to the fittest and that an
accommodating Providence ensures the fittest are as a rule found in
the upper and middle classes.

The late Anthony Crosland drew what seems to me to be a valid
distinction between the weak and strong definition of equal opportunity. The weak definition is that children of equal measured intelligence should have the same start in life. In Britain even according
to the weak definition, we have fallen far short of equal opportunity.
No amount of propaganda can hide that ugly fact. The English
public schools and their Scottish equivalents to all intents and

purposes remain closed to the poorest children, however clever. Those who are able to buy private education have a distinct advantage in securing entrance to the two privileged citadels of learning: Oxford and Cambridge.

The strong definition of equal opportunity is that, subject to differences in heredity, every child should have the same chance of acquiring measured intelligence as far as this can be controlled by social action. The implications of the strong definition of equal opportunity are radical in the extreme. Taken seriously it would mean the creation of a new society where bad housing, bad incomes, badly educated parents, are eliminated. The weak definition of equal opportunity invariably goes hand in hand with a *laissez-faire* market outlook.

In Edinburgh, perhaps the most educationally élitist city in the British Isles, my two sons, Alasdair and Alan, went to comprehensive state schools. The congregation of St. George's West was shocked, but, bless them, they remained loyal and supportive to the end. There was a good deal of sniping from friends and critics alike. 'Isn't it your bounden duty to do the best for your children?' they would truculently ask me. My answer to this as a rule evoked blank incomprehension: 'I am a preacher and every week I proclaim the most radical of all doctrines under the sun, "The Fatherhood of God". This implies I must implacably oppose educational segregation. Reinhold Neibuhr is right. The family is the most selfless and at the same time the most selfish of all human groups.'

Reading, I would claim, is one of my most pleasant and rewarding concerns. It began at primary school and has continued ever since. According to American research most university and college products give up serious reading within a few years of graduating. This is tragic. It spits in the face of the meaning of education. A university and college education is only the aperitif, whetting our appetite for the main course. There comes a time when we can dispense with our tutors and take up the serious business of educating ourselves.

A preacher's reading must be as comprehensive as it is humanly possible. He or she must keep abreast of what is happening in philosophy, theology, psychology and science. We live in a world shaped, if not indeed dominated, by science. As most ministers, with notable exceptions, are not trained in science, they must rely to some extent on lucid expositors. It is my conviction that there is none better than the late Arthur Koestler. We shall learn much about astro-physics, psychology, neuro-physiology and politics if we read his *Ghost in the Machine, Janus, Act of Creation*, and the greatest political novel of the twentieth century, *Darkness at Noon*.

For the preacher reading is not a luxury, it is a basic necessity. It is not possible to proclaim the gospel, week after week, month after month, year after year, in any relevant sense unless we commune with the original thinkers and creative writers of our day. What is more, reading has considerable utilitarian value. In the business of preaching it is grist to the mill, providing the preacher with an inexhaustible mine of illustrative material. John Milton described a good book as 'the precious life blood of a man's spirit'. Thomas Carlyle, the craggy sage, put it thus: 'All that mankind has done, thought, gained or been, it is lying in magic preservation in the pages of books.'

Fascination with the paranormal I would also include among my concerns. I share this interest with my provocative preacher journalist friend, Steward Lamont. My conversion from sceptical undergraduate arrogance to an unwavering allegiance to the study of the paranormal was truly dramatic. While still a student at St. Andrews University, I spent the long summer holidays at home in the Isle of Harris. One lovely August afternoon I was helping my father cut the corn, when Alasdair MacKinnon, a crofter who lived a mile or so away, on his way back from the village shop, stopped to speak to us. He invited me to a ceilidh in his home. Later on, after I had taken off my working clothes and washed, the two of us walked along a footpath on the edge of a beautiful loch.

Without warning it happened. Alasdair stopped in his tracks. His face underwent an indescribable change. He began to shiver. Big globules of sweat stood out on his brow. He whispered in a kind of strange, strangled voice, 'Calum is dead.' I knew who he was referring to. Calum was his son who had emigrated to Canada some twelve years before. I grasped Alasdair by the elbow, steadied him and helped him home. For the rest of the evening he did not utter one word. Round about noon next day the postman called at our house and said to my mother, 'Isn't it sad about Calum MacKinnon?' 'What happened?' she asked. 'He was killed yesterday in Montreal,' was the answer. Later we calculated the time difference. Calum's death coincided uncannily with Alasdair's strange psychic experience.

More than once in Edinburgh, Stirling and Glasgow, I have had direct experience of poltergeist phenomena, puzzling, sometimes frightening. On two occasions, accompanied by my friend, Professor Bill Shaw, I have taken part in services of exorcism which appeared to prove successful. I am not sure. The energy behind these inexplicable disturbances may have been on the point of petering out when Bill and I stepped in.

Since then I have read many books on the paranormal. They play sheer havoc with our traditional understanding of cause and effect. How do we explain Alasdair MacKinnon's awareness of his son's death? Was it telepathy, precognition or clairvoyance? Frankly I don't know, but of this I am absolutely certain. The perversity of modern physics and the evidence for psychic communication may not have a profound religious significance, but between them they have utterly discredited an old-fashioned materialism and a Newtonian mechanistic universe.

All these interests I have found exciting, but by far the most compelling of all my concerns is the communication of the Christian gospel.

Theology used to be accepted as the Queen of the Sciences. It may have lost a lot of its former prestige, but it is still an important discipline. All our problems are at bottom theological ones. So was slavery. So is apartheid. So is every injustice that robs men and women of their God-given dignity.

The preacher must be hospitable to the insights of the great theologians. He will listen attentively to Barth, to Bultmann, to Bonhoeffers, to Baillie, to Niebuhr, to Tillich and to Multmann. His or her task is to take their insights, strip them of abstractions, clothe them in vivid imagery and idiom and communicate them persuasively from the pulpit. Not an easy task but an exhilarating one!

A staunch ally of theology is modern existentialist literature. Sartre, Camus, Millar, Golding and Ian Crichton Smith, Derick Thomson, Norman MacCaig and others may be agnostics, but this they have in common with the theologians, that they take the human predicament seriously. And some of them wrestle with it more robustly and more sensitively than many preachers.

On the whole much of modern evangelism depresses me. American millionaire televangelists have sordidly devalued the Christian faith by harnessing it to a free-for-all profit-making capitalism. To very complex questions they deliberately and dishonestly give simplistic answers. Worst of all, many of them have sanctified their voracious acquisitiveness in the name of Jesus Christ.

I do not claim to be a born-again Christian, though I fully accept that there are those who can genuinely make that claim. The nearest I have ever come to this enviable experience was in the moral philosophy classroom when that brilliant philosopher, Reginald Jackson, was expounding the 'Ethics' of the atheist John Stuart Mill. One sentence in the book leapt out and hit me with sledge-hammer force: 'I can only believe in a God who is better than myself.' For me this proved a kind of Damascus-road experience. On my way home to my lodgings I said goodbye to the neurotic, life-denying God, who is opposed to healthy sport, uplifting secular music and the ordination of women as elders and ministers.

There are ministers and lay people who claim that the outbreak of AIDS is a Divine Judgement. God lost his patience with a lascivious and promiscuous generation, so he sent this scourge worse than the Black Death to teach us a lesson. How can any decent, intelligent man or woman bow the knee to such a cosmic, mindless sadist? I am not saying this monstrous Deity is proclaimed from all our pulpits, but he is from some of them.

If the Christian Church is to survive we must preach a God who is better than ourselves, in sum, God the Father of our Lord Jesus Christ. He is infinitely more intelligent than the most brilliant among us, infinitely more compassionate than the purest of the saints, infinitely more involved in the human predicament than the most outrageous of all radicals. Isn't that the meaning of the Incarnation? If we are really serious about evangelism, we must not preach a God who is morally inferior to ourselves.

If we are to communicate the gospel meaningfully we must take preaching seriously. Let us create a generation of preachers who will emulate Laurence Olivier with his incomparable skills as an actor. This calls for hard work, determination and great sensitivity. The preacher's task is not just demanding – it is frightening. He or she is called to proclaim in word and action the authentic marks of the Christian Faith.

One authentic mark is critical reflection, hence the importance of theology. Critical inquiry belongs to the Divine Image within us. It is no respecter of persons. It recognises no sanctified precincts, no sacred niches, no holy of holies. Over our pretentions and posturings it stands like a flaming angel. It is the sworn enemy of mushy sentimentality.

Another authentic mark is human compassion. The Apostle Paul is right. Love is the supreme gift. Compassion is not a disembodied theological abstraction. It is always incarnate and always costly. Love means relationships which involve risk and hurt. Love knows no bounds. It embraces the whole of humanity. The black man is neither my ward nor my case, he is the image of myself in which I experience the agony of belonging. The prostitute is neither my case nor my campaign. She is the incarnation of my sale of true selfhood. The saint is neither my idol nor my reproach. Kagawa of Japan and Mother Teresa are not my accusers, they are the challenge urging me to unearth the Divine Image buried deep within my nature.

Finally there is the authentic mark of a redeeming and reconciling community.

What is the number one threat to the survival of the human race upon this planet? Is it the hydrogen bomb? Certainly not! The hydrogen bomb is neuter. Of its own volition it can't press the fatal button. No! The real threat is the fact of proximity without community. Science has forced proximity upon us whether we like it or not. We can have a breakfast in London, then step aboard the Concorde and have a second breakfast in New York, one hour before the one we consumed in London. That is proximity.

But Community! Dear God it seems a million light years away. We can control objects orbiting in outer space, but we cannot control

Northern Ireland. We can land men on the moon, but it took us forty years to cross from East to West Berlin. Yes! Without any shadow of doubt our most deadly enemy is the fact of proximity without community.

Margaret Thatcher, the longest serving Prime Minister of this century, is on record in saying, 'There is no such thing as Society; it is made up of individuals.' She was abysmally wrong. The truth is that Society is more than an aggregate of individuals; It is also made up of basic philosophies, unexamined assumptions, entrenched prejudices, which between them are capable of denying the Brotherhood of Man.

The God who has addressed us so unambiguously in Jesus Christ, will not allow self-appointed reactionaries to thwart his invincible purpose in history. Authentic religion is not a private, esoteric, individualistic affair. It is rooted in social solidarity. God acts through individual lives. Of course he does. He also acts through social and political structures. Christian commitment is first and foremost commitment to Christ, but commitment to him carries with it an unyielding resolve to create a healing community transcending our mutual alienations and antagonisms.

# Chapter 15

# The Law, the Word and the Head of the Kirk

## Lord Mackay of Clashfern

*James Peter Mackay (Lord Mackay of Clashfern), Lord Chancellor of Great Britain, provides a fitting epilogue to this volume, first delivered as the St. Cuthbert Lecture on Church and State and reprinted from* Life and Work. *Lord Mackay has his roots in Caithness within the Free Presbyterian tradition and was a gracious ambassador for this small but vigorous Calvinist Church until his attendance at a Roman Catholic funeral mass for a fellow judge precipitated an irreconcilable split within the denomination. While remaining sympathetic to the more liberal wing (now the APC Church) he has remained above the fray, a characteristic that has served him well in his role as principal law officer in both Scotland and England for the Conservative government during a decade of change. His unique achievement, to have served as both Lord Advocate and Lord Chancellor, gives him a unique perspective on the British State, in which the role of the established churches has increasingly come under question.*

It can be said, I think, that the Church of Scotland is established by law but I am sure it would be quite wrong to say that the authority for the Church's existence is that it was established by law. On the contrary, the whole history of the Church's position and claims suggests that it was because Parliament recognized the authority of the Church that it was accorded this particular status in law.

The authority of the Church in matters spiritual is thoroughly recognized, not only by Parliament but also by the courts. This attitude so far as the courts are concerned extends to other churches than the Church of Scotland itself. The courts do not take upon themselves the responsibility of deciding upon matters of faith. They may have to decide as matter of fact what were the beliefs of a particular organization at a particular time as these beliefs may define the constitution of the organization for whose benefit monies are held in trust.

The authority of the Church of Scotland was recognized by Parliament as coming from the head, the Lord Jesus Christ. Just as, by him kings reign and princes decree justice, in the language of the Westminster Confession of Faith 'there is no other head of the Church but the Lord Jesus Christ'.

## One Head

So far as the Church of Scotland is concerned, there is no question of the Queen being its head in any sense whatsoever. The Church of Scotland acknowledges no head but the Lord Jesus Christ alone. Thus, we see two forms of authority co-existing; the authority of Her Majesty to rule and administer justice derived from God and the authority of the Church to rule in matters spiritual derived from God. Neither subordinate in its own sphere to the other, distinct so far as human authority is concerned and yet the authority for each flowing ultimately from the same divine source.

These distinct types of authority have very different characteristics. The authority to rule and administer justice conferred upon kings and princes is of a coercive character. Obedience to their rules and orders is enforced by sanctions, civil and criminal, and it may be encouraged by rewards. In the spiritual domain, while the Church has sanctions available to it in the shape of regulating those who may partake of its communion or hold office in the Church, the purpose of the Church's existence is to win the hearts of people for its head.

## Basis of Love

The morality which the Bible teaches may be summed up in these two great commandments on which hang all the law and the prophets; thou shalt love the Lord thy God with all thine heart, with all thy soul, with all thy strength and with all thy mind and they neighbour as thyself. Love, although it appears in commandments is something which cannot be forced or coerced. In so far as authority is thought of as coercive it cannot be the basis of a morality founded upon love.

The authority of the Church accordingly is pre-eminently an authority to persuade; an authority to call for a willing, hearty obedience, not an enforced obedience.

In its administration the Church has courts, kirk session, presbytery, provincial Synod and General Assembly and each of these has authority over those subordinate to it in the hierarchy. But these courts are not absolute with freedom to legislate as they wish. It is true that they are not subject in matters spiritual to any earthly authority but the very reason for their existence is the acknowledgement of the authority of the head of the Church and the supreme and only rule by which they should be regulated is the holy scriptures received as God's word.

I said earlier that the authority of the House of Commons to legislate is derived from its election. But the authority once granted lasts for a period up to five years. After election the House of Commons could so act and perhaps particularly the government representing the ruling party or the party having the majority could so act as to alienate the support of those who voted for it. In this way, while it might continue to have formal authority, it might well lose real authority to continue legislating. Although the position in the United States of America is very different constitutionally from ours we have an illustration, a sad illustration in the recent past, of a president elected with resounding acclaim who by his actions subsequent to election lost the authority to continue. Authority in this important sense carries with it the idea of agreement with and honour and respect for, the person holding authority.

## Test of Experience

When Parliament is seen to be doing something which I know to be right, it has, for me, an authority much greater, more compelling than is accorded merely by the fact that I, along with many others, voted those MPs into the House. This is, I believe, the authority referred to that Jesus possessed as distinct from the scribes. His pronouncements carried with them a conviction of their truth in the minds of the hearers. This above all is the authority we need today.

On matters connected with the affairs of government of the nation one of the tests from which authority may be derived is the test of actual experience. If a particular policy given a reasonable amount of time does not produce the result that its proponents have claimed for it their claims are bound to be weakened in the judgement of impartial people. It may well be that we are seeing the claims of the permissive society for the happiness of freedom from restraint being put to just such a test and a very sad test in the present threat of the plague of AIDS. The rules of conduct which those who advocate permissiveness delight to abandon may well be founded in a much deeper reality than they have yet realized.

As I have said, the only authority for faith and life that the Church of Scotland has historically recognized is God's word – the Bible. In so far as it has had subordinate standards they have had authority only because they were received as properly based upon the Bible. But as the Bible is the authority in the Church so, in my judgement, it is the authority of the Church. The Church has no authority to require reception of any other authority. The Church cannot ask me to accept Professor X's opinion or Dr Y's opinion. Surely, the Church must follow the example of its head when challenged. How often do we find him saying 'it is written'? The fact that the only authority on which the Church can properly rely and whose reception it alone can advocate is that of God speaking in his word in no way prevents her from the most diligent, eloquent and persuasive explanation of that word. Dr Y and Professor X may use their full talent and great education in showing me and guiding me to the true meaning of that word and if I follow them in their explanations of it, I shall more fully get the message of it myself.

We live in an age in which science has made great strides. Understanding has been gained of many phenomena which were utterly mysterious to our forefathers. This has not been matched, in my view, by any comparable progress in the understanding of man's spirit, of the aim and purpose of his life or of what lies beyond death. It is these matters that the Church has authority to address; authority conferred by the Master by that commission which he gave after his resurrection: 'Go ye into all the world and preach the gospel to every creature.'

## Love and Law

It is that gospel which is capable of transforming men's spirits and of giving them that love which is the fulfilling of the law, enabling them to respond heartily to the one who said: 'If ye love me keep my commandments.'

When we cast off the authority of God we cast off with it all human authority. Insofar as we are able to pursue that policy we create utter disorder in the society in which we live. I believe the Church's authority is to call us by God's word to come unto him through Jesus Christ in faith and in repentance accepting him as our Lord. When we do so every other authority subordinate to him will have its proper place in our allegiance. When we are reconciled to God through Christ his law will become a law of liberty to us to serve him fully, heartily, always. There will be perfect freedom and among the many activities that we shall be called upon to perform is that: 'To pray for kings and for all that are in authority that we may lead a quiet and peaceable life in all godliness and honesty.'

In 1985 the Board of Social Responsibility of the Church of Scotland completed an analysis of a lifestyle survey which they took covering members of the Church of Scotland, of the Roman Catholic Church and of other churches. Amongst many matters disclosed by that analysis it is disturbing to learn that 69 per cent of Church of Scotland members seldom or never read their Bible, only a tiny proportion, 7.3 per cent did so every day, while a somewhat larger but still small proportion of 25 per cent did so in the other church group and 4.3 per cent did so in the Roman Catholics' group. If, as I believe, the reason for the Church's existence is to proclaim the Bible and its teaching in the world, it is a sad reflection on how ineffectively that is being carried out when these figures are disclosed in such a survey of the Churches.

I believe every one of us has a deep responsibility to examine where we stand in this matter. What really is our faith? Whose authority do we, as individuals, recognize? Are we adherents of the Church and its witness in name only or do we, personally, receive Jesus Christ as our Lord and Saviour? Do we accept his word as our only rule of faith and life? Do we seek to live by it and do we seek to promote its witness by our own lives?

Only when we do so shall we know true authority in our lives and only then will all the other authorities, who have a claim on our allegiance, present a coherent pattern to us of how we should live in a contented society.

## Other Books by Stewart Lamont

*Religion Inc*
(an exposé of Scientology)

*Is Anybody There?*
(a study of the paranormal)

*Church and State – Uneasy Alliances*

*The Swordbearer*
(a major assessment of John Knox)

*In Good Faith*
(a selection of his Saturday column
contributions to the *Herald*)